The Historical Series of the Reformed Church
in America
No. 3

PIONEERS
IN THE
ARAB WORLD

by

DOROTHY F. VAN ESS

WM. B. EERDMANS PUBLISHING CO.
GRAND RAPIDS, MICHIGAN

Dorothy F. Van Ess

Library of Congress Cataloging in Publication Data

Van Ess, Dorothy, F.
  Pioneers in the Arab world.

  (The Historical series of the Reformed Church in
America, no. 3)
    Bibliography: pp. 187-88
    1. Van Ess, Dorothy. 2. Van Ess, John, 1879-1949
  3. Missions to Muslims—Basrah. I. Title. II. Series:
Reformed church in America. The historical series,
no. 3.
  BV2626.V36A36   266'.5'7320924 [B]   74-14964
  ISBN 0-8028-1585-5

To
Reformed Church Women
for the
100th Anniversary of the Women's Board of Foreign Missions

Printed in the United States of America

Contents

Illustrations

The Historical Series of the Reformed Church in America

This series has been inaugurated by the General Synod of the Reformed Church in America, acting through its Commission on History, for the purpose of encouraging historical research and providing a medium wherein this knowledge may be shared with the academic community and with the members of the denomination in order that a knowledge of the past may contribute to right action in the present.

Editor

The Rev. Donald J. Bruggink, Ph.D., Western Theological Seminary

Editor's Preface

Pioneers in the Arab World is the first volume of the Historical Series of the Reformed Church in America in the genre of autobiographical history. The vitality of this book will convince many that we should henceforth eschew all heavily footnoted histories and specialize in first-person documentaries. Whenever the Historical Commission can find people who have been at the center of the history of their times (as were John and Dorothy Van Ess) and have a flair for exciting narrative (as has Dorothy) their efforts will not be overlooked, or unpublished.

The importance of the Arabian Mission of the Reformed Church was not confined to the area of religion. The Christianity of its missionaries was deeply rooted in all of life, and the result was an impact on education, health, and the structures of society. Dorothy Van Ess called to my attention a quotation from Sir Arnold Wilson, formerly High Commissioner in Iraq and for many years active in political affairs in the Persian Gulf, who in a lecture before the Royal Geographic Society in London in 1927 offered the following observation on missions:

I should not like to speak about the Persian Gulf without bearing testimony to the wonderful work the missionaries are doing. . . . The Arab is a Muhammadan first and an Arab after, like all Islamic races; he regards Europeans likewise as Christians first and foremost. . . . He does not despise but greatly respects those who devote their lives to spreading by example and teaching, the Christian religion. There is no greater influence for good in the Persian Gulf than the Christian Missions; no Europeans are so universally respected as are the missionaries such as Zwemer, Van Ess, Harrison, and Mylrea—and those who decry foreign missions do less than justice to themselves and harm to our good name.

This testimony from the decade of the twenties is buttressed by the American journalist, Jerome Beatty of the *American Magazine*, who in the late thirties did a series of articles on the ten most important Americans abroad. While his interests included statesmen and businessmen as well as journalists and the religious, the Reformed Church in America found itself contributing three names to this august list of ten: Dr. Ida Scudder, Dr. Paul W. Harrison, and Dr. John Van Ess. After his interview with John Van Ess, Mr. Beatty left Basrah for Bombay, and during the trip remembered that he had not asked Van Ess as to how many converts he had made. Sending a wire from Bombay he soon received John's reply: "Only Allah knows."

Acknowledgments must be made to the Reformed Church Women for their cooperation in the publication of this volume, and especially to the Rev. Sharon T. Scholten for his perceptive editorial comments, to Ms. Nancy Van Wyk and Mr. Milo Van Veldhuizen who read galley and page proofs, and to Dr. John W. Beardslee III and Miss Elsie Stryker, who prepared the bibliography, both of materials relating to the Arabian Mission and to the works of John and Dorothy Van Ess.

Donald J. Bruggink
Western Theological Seminary
Holland, Michigan

Foreword

One of the earliest recollections I have of Dorothy Van Ess is the sight of a tall, erect, beautifully costumed woman passing my office door at the Reformed Church headquarters, then located at 156 Fifth Avenue in New York City. She was doing research for the writing of her earlier book and for the history of the Arabian Mission and needed to search the files of the Board of Foreign Missions.

I had come to New York in late 1953 for an assignment with the Board of Domestic Missions. Although I found the Reformed Church mission and ministry on the North American Continent to be exciting and the work satisfying, yet the overseas program had an interest and an intrigue about it which was accentuated by the "doings" of Mrs. Van Ess as she plied her way through papers, pictures and portfolios.

Study tours in 1958 and 1969 introduced me to the mysteries and miracles of mission in the Far East and Asia, but it was in 1972 that the Middle East names and places became real to me. Organizing and coordinating a "Middle East Journey" hosted by Ruth and Ed Luidens, I joined in a memorable visit to those stations so vividly described by Dorothy in this volume.

Ruth and Rachel Jackson, Cornelia Dalenberg, Ruth and Ed Luidens, Amy Zwemer Violette, "Monti" Johnson (formerly Mrs. Paul Harrison), Mrs. Richard Zwemer (niece of Dr. Samuel) were members of this company which met old friends, enjoyed audience with sheikh and sheikah, and recalled familiar incidents and happenings in the history of the Reformed Church mission in the Middle East. How much it would have meant to have had Dorothy Van Ess with us!

During that journey and again as I have read her story, I was impressed with the strength and greatness of those early pioneers. Characteristic of both men and women was a courageous and adventuresome spirit, political astuteness, academic excellence, social awareness, and unbounded physical energy. I heard, saw, and felt, time and again the complete and unswerving commitment to their task. Evident was the deep concern for their families. At the same time one could see how they cherished and guarded the right to be private persons and to engage in a personal pilgrimage. Clear, too, was the contentment known only to and experienced by those who have Christ and His cause as the focus of their lives.

"Deep in the heart of each member of the Arabian Mission has always been a sense of imperativeness to the point of thralldom and yet with it a sense of emancipation that comes with the consciousness of being held by an irresistible and ultimately triumphant idea," so said John Van Ess after the founding of the Arabian Mission, and with those words I believe one can still describe the conviction and challenge one finds in the missionary movement.

It is altogether fitting that this book be published as the women of the Reformed Church join in celebrating the 100th anniversary of the organization of the Women's Board of Foreign Missions. Dorothy Van Ess was intimately related to the purpose and program of that Board, indeed at one point serving as its interim secretary.

Some months ago Dorothy Van Ess and I shared in a mission presentation. Still tall, erect, beautifully costumed, and articulate in her faith and fervor for mission, she stirred the minds and hearts of young and old. So, too, does *Pioneers in the Arab World*.

Beth E. Marcus
Executive Director
Reformed Church Women

Introduction

An introduction of Dorothy and John Van Ess is superfluous, as this volume serves admirably for an introduction to them both. Through them, the reader will also be introduced to a very significant segment of modern history, not only a view of the twentieth century church in mission, but of the emergence of one of the many "new nations" whose birth has been one of the major events of recent world history. Some of the setting that Iraq provided for the lives of the Van Esses should be stated, both from the viewpoint of church activity and of general history.

One of the greatest achievements of the Christian Church in the nineteenth century—probably its greatest achievement—was in the amazing growth of the "foreign missionary" movement, which enjoyed what Professor Latourette rightly taught us to regard as its "great century." Protestantism in particular was profoundly changed by its rapid awakening to an awareness of world-wide responsibility and world-wide opportunity. Roman Catholicism also, with its older tradition of world-wide concern and activity, experienced a renewal of missionary life on a broader base than ever before.

Today, hindsight enables us to recognize that much of the geographical and numerical growth of Christianity, especially in the century between the downfall of Napoleon and the outbreak of the first World War, was the result of the movement of the spirit of the times as much as of the Spirit of God. Leaders in "backward" nations (later to be called "undeveloped" and more recently "developing"), often humiliated by military defeat, saw Christianity in the manner of many triumphant Europeans and Americans, as the religious phase of "Western civilization," and as the key to development and social progress—to the acquiring of highly desired materialistic standards, and of political equality. Many mistakes were made by the missionaries. John Van Ess's own attitude toward British military and colonial power partook of the realities of a past generation—realities that our generation should understand although we can no

longer experience them—and no doubt partook also of the
illusions of that generation. But it survived the disappointments
of the aftermath of a "war to end war," and the shock of the
collapse of the securities on which it had leaned, because it was
grounded in a reality quite other than the triumphs of the white
man.

Wendell Wilkie, after discovering that mankind lives in one
world, paid homage to Christian missionaries for their part in
that world, describing them as persons devoted to truth. High as
that praise is, it misses the mark. The missionaries were divided
by a myriad of theological emphases, all of them resulting from
efforts to speak the truth. They were united in their loyalty,
not to any abstraction, but to Jesus Christ—Way, Truth, and
Life—the only remedy they recognized for the sin of mankind
and the evil of the world. In this loyalty they multiplied the
number of believers, witnessed to the ends of the earth, built
new institutions, transformed and humanized old cultures, and
planted new churches that still carry on the saving work, even
though the foreigner is often now excluded from leadership.

John and Dorothy Van Ess are exemplars in the first rank of
this loyalty to Jesus Christ and witness to Him in "distant
places," this glory of modern church history. This "introduction" is penned by one who played a brief and minor role
abroad in partnership with them, whose talents were guided by
them as part of a great whole, and whose weaknesses were part
of the cross they bore with patience. It was a privilege to serve
with them. It is a joy to see their story told in the form that is
now set forth—of Dorothy's memory of their life together and
the mark that it made on one nation.

The world of Islam, toward the end of the nineteenth century, was the great exception to the rule that this was an age of
triumphant missionary expansion. Except for Judaism, Islam
has the greatest resemblance to Christianity of any of the great
religions and has had the most intimate relations to it over the
centuries. Those relations have been marked by bitter conflict,
by the Muslim's sense of superiority, and by his successful
resistance to evangelization. The cultural and military glories of
Islam had become part of the distant past, and most Muslims
lived in subjection to the great "Christian" empires, but even in
the 1890s and early 1900s Turkey, "sick man of Europe"
though she might be, was an empire, ruling over Christians as
well as Muslims, in Europe as well as in Asia, and the ordinary

Muslim was not only proud of his faith, but convinced of his spiritual superiority. The Islamic world had never lacked a Christian presence, but Christians, although permitted to educate their children and guaranteed by religious law the right to practice their faith, were relegated to the status of second class citizens and were strictly forbidden to make converts. In Iraq, where the Van Ess story would take place, as in other Arab lands, they were isolated from the main currents of Christendom for centuries, with very limited educational opportunities, and largely untouched by the spiritual movements that had remade the churches of Europe and America. Roman Catholic and Protestant missionaries, almost universally frustrated in efforts to convert Muslims, had done some very significant work in revitalizing segments of the old Christian communities of the Near East. The work of American Congregationalists and Presbyterians, for several generations, among the "Nestorians" near Lake Urmia in Persia might be mentioned here because of the role immigrants from that region eventually played in the little evangelical community of Iraq, and the United Presbyterian missions in Syria and Egypt belong to this story since the son of one of these missionaries, John G. Lansing, became a professor at New Brunswick Seminary, brought his concern for the Islamic world into the Reformed Church, and guided the formation of the Arabian Mission. But the "Christian presence" in the Arab world did not become an evangelistic force, and Arabia proper, "The cradle of Islam," was unique in the Muslim world, first because the sacredness of the city of Mecca and the great annual pilgrimage gave this otherwise "backward" area a place of first importance in the Islamic consciousness, and secondly because there, alone among Islamic countries, Christians had been expelled once and for all in the formative days of the faith, and the Christian voice, muted everywhere that Islam had gone, was silent in Arabia.

Such was the situation at the end of the 1880s when James Cantine and Samuel Zwemer entered New Brunswick Seminary, and in the early 1890s when, having combined their missionary enthusiasms with the more seasoned vision of Professor Lansing, they had determined on a new foreign missionary enterprise, one designed to reach the Arabs through the Arabian heartland. The vision has not yet been achieved, and Mecca is still unreached. In 1974, the press is reporting the possible purchase of a French luxury liner for the transportation of many thousands of the Muslim worshippers who visit the city that has yet to receive a single Christian missionary. But the young men who formulated the vision were not easily discouraged, and never allowed any series of frustrations to turn them back. Refused support by the Board of Foreign Missions, they, with Professor Lansing and others, formed a new mission board, the Arabian Syndicate, which was eventually taken over by the Reformed Church but which initially financed and promoted the new venture. Denied admission to the mainland of Arabia, they ventured into the Persian Gulf, and, as one of their main centers, chose the port of Basrah, on the great river formed by the confluence of the storied streams of Mesopotamia, the Tigris and Euphrates.

Here was to be the scene of the Van Ess story, and Dorothy must tell it. Perhaps we need to be reminded that Basrah and the rest of Iraq in 1903 were among the Arab provinces of the Turkish empire. The imperialism under which Arabs were then restless was that of their Muslim brethren, the Turks, and the revolution of the "Young Turks" at Constantinople favored Turkish nationalism rather than empire-wide reform and Arab aspiration. World War I would see Turkey as a German ally and as the source of some major disasters to British arms—the Dardenelles, Gallipoli, Kut—but in the end the Turkish empire was a defeated power. Out of her ruins sprang a new nationalist republic, while her Arab provinces became the responsibility of an unprepared League of Nations, and Iraq, under the guidance of the dying British Empire, sought to assume her place among sovereign nations. It was in the midst of the still uncompleted birth agonies of this nation that the bulk of the Van Ess's lives was lived. They came as part of a vision that sought to evangelize the Arabs from their own spiritual center. Prevented from doing things in their own way, they and their colleagues never wavered in their determination to show Christ to Muslims. Dorothy tells the story in her own way, with inadequate reference to her own achievements, but as she tells it her own part becomes clear.

By telling many specifics about the lives of two missionaries and of their Arab friends, she has shown us much of the inner meaning of the missionary movement and of its significance for the world, and for the churches that supported it.

More than some denominations, the Reformed Church in America has been shaped by its foreign program, which for generations was a major emphasis and a point of common loyalty for the very diverse and geographically separated sections of the church. In its mission work it was proud to use the talents of many who, like Dorothy Van Ess, did not grow up within it. Congregationalists, Presbyterians, and Anglicans were appointed to the Arabian mission, but that mission became and remained what it was through the lives of Reformed Church people from all sections of the denomination. Through missionaries, and through none more than those of the Arabian Mission, the small denomination became known to, and respected by, thousands who otherwise would never have heard of it— undergraduates, noted scholars, political administrators, and explorers, as well as churchmen around the world. Above all, myriads of people were introduced to Christ, and many Muslims at last were convinced that there were Christians worthy of respect. Two of these missionaries speak together in Dorothy's book.

John W. Beardslee III
Professor of Church History
New Brunswick Theological Seminary

I
Meeting on the Sand

A self-willed donkey threw me from his back onto the sand when I had been in Arabia one week. It was at a picnic tea, a special treat arranged for the benefit of the new missionaries of whom I was one.

A daughter of New England, I had left the security of an instructor's desk in a college classroom to be a pioneer in women's education in the Arab world. My initiation into a strange new existence was making rapid progress.

Today we were to go to one of the beauty spots on the island of Bahrain, an old Portuguese fort up the seashore.

"How are we getting there?" I inquired apprehensively from one of the older missionaries.

"Oh, we're riding on donkeys," was the breezy reply.

My heart sank when I heard of the proposed transportation, for we had come ashore on donkeys on our arrival, and I had realized that there would never be any "rapport" between myself and these useful beasts. The mail steamer on which we had traveled up from Bombay to Bahrain had to anchor miles offshore. We and all our belongings went down a precarious ship's ladder into large sailboats and proceeded to sail for several hours toward shore. Once there it was low tide and the boats couldn't get near enough to the rocks, which were the landing place, for us to disembark. We were hoisted unceremoniously onto the backs of donkeys for the final stage of our journey. I acquired a deep distrust of donkeys on that occasion but I tried to join lightheartedly in the pleasure jaunt on my first Saturday and had no premonition of what a fateful day it was in my life.

The time was early January, 1910, and the place was Bahrain, an island on the Arabian side of the Persian Gulf. Today everyone has heard of the little oil-rich Sheikhdom just across a narrow strait from the mighty Kingdom of Saudi Arabia but fifty years ago it was poor and unimportant and practically unknown. Its chief claim to renown was that it was one of the world centers of the pearl industry.

The occasion was the annual meeting of the mission I had just joined, the Arabian Mission of the Reformed Church in America. The founders of the mission were Dr. Samuel Zwemer and Dr. James Cantine, graduates of the New Brunswick Theological Seminary of the Reformed Church in New Brunswick, New Jersey. They were loyal sons of the old Dutch traditions and filled with pioneer spirit. They had visited American missions in Syria (including Lebanon) and Egypt, and the Keith Falconer Mission of the Church of Scotland in Aden, while making up their minds as to where to open new work in the Arab world, and decided to begin work with Muslims in lower Mesopotamia and the Arabian side of the Persian Gulf. The Church Missionary Society of the Church of England was working in the north in Mosul and Baghdad, but there was no Christian witness south of that.

In 1889 they began, and the accounts by both Cantine and Zwemer of their early journeyings around Arabia, their perils and adventures, are truly apostolic. In his later days Dr. Zwemer earned the title "Apostle to Islam" for he travelled widely throughout the whole Muslim world and became an authority on Islam. By the time I joined the mission in 1909, the work was well established in three centers: Basrah, in the Turkish province which later became Iraq; Bahrain, an island in the Persian Gulf; and Muscat, in the Sultanate of Oman.

I was very fortunate in my first journey to Arabia, for I travelled all the way from New York to Bahrain under the wing of Dr. James Cantine and his wife. Our senior mission founder was a distinguished figure in his clerical dress and his wife was a gentlewoman of quiet charm and grace. I felt proud to belong to them. We were joined in Trieste by three other new missionaries: Dr. Christine Iverson, who had been paying a visit to relatives in Denmark, and Edwin and Eleanor Calverley, who had been honeymooning in Europe.

Eleanor was also a doctor and was later to begin medical work for women in Kuwait after it became a station of the mission. Edwin was a clergyman, and was to become an outstanding Arabic and Islamic scholar, concluding his active career as head of the Kennedy School of Missions in Hartford, Connecticut.

On a comfortable Lloyd Trestino ship we voyaged down the Adriatic, across the Mediterranean, through the Suez Canal and down the Red Sea, and then crossed the Indian Ocean to

Bombay. Dr. Cantine gave us Arabic lessons every day as we sat on deck in the balmy air enjoying the blue skies and still bluer seas. We had all learned to read by the time we came to the end of our journey and could repeat the Lord's Prayer in Arabic and venture a few halting sentences.

In Bombay we spent some days lodging pleasantly at the old Great Western Hotel, saw friends, explored the fascinating city, and did necessary shopping. Christine and I had never slept under mosquito nets before, and we discovered in the middle of our first night that we were both lying wide awake. So we got into one bed together and talked a great deal and slept a little. But what I chiefly remember about our first night in India is how harrowed we both were by the distressing coughing of an Indian in the courtyard below our balcony. Christine was sure he was in the last stages of galloping consumption, and told me energetically,

"In the morning, the first thing I shall do will be to see that that poor man gets medical care."

We discovered that coughing and spitting were one of the Indian coolie's few joys and were seldom serious.

We had to buy mosquito nets and camp beds, and also "Punkah lamps." These latter were fitted with special tops which kept them from being extinguished by the breeze of the hand-pulled ceiling punkahs, which were the forerunners of electric fans.

We obediently bought other things which Mrs. Cantine told us were necessary, and had a strange assortment of boxes and bundles, in addition to our neat American luggage, when we boarded the British India ship "Kola." This was the "fass" mail which would take us to Karachi and Muscat. From there it went directly up the Persian Gulf to Bushire and Basrah, so we had to transship to the slow mail at Muscat. Here we saw our first mission station and were joined by Dr. and Mrs. Sharon Thoms and their three delightful children. Mrs. Thoms and Mrs. Cantine were sisters so it was a joyful reunion. On our first day on the old S. S. "Belimba," which was to take us to Bahrain, a sailor produced a jellyfish, and small Wells Thoms proceeded to cut it up. Recently I have seen a film in which Dr. Wells Thoms, an experienced and senior mission doctor, performed a delicate eye operation, and to my mind came instantly a vivid picture of the little boy squatting on the deck of a B. I. ship, solemnly and intently dissecting a jellyfish.

On the Gulf we steamed for several blue and gold days, stopping at ports on both sides, Arabian and Persian, where we were entranced with the country boats with their vociferous passengers, and their fearful and wonderful baggage. For fifteen rupees (then about five dollars) I bought a Persian rug from a pilgrim bound for the Shiah Muslim shrines in Mesopotamia. I still cherish it and its associations.

At length at the very end of the year 1909 we reached Bahrain. The missionaries from Basrah had already arrived so the meeting was officially organized as soon as we were all settled. At this yearly get-together the far-flung members of the mission transacted their business, reported on their activities, and planned for the future. But perhaps the greatest benefit of all was the companionship afforded by these gatherings.

During the first week, when we "missionary freshmen" sat in on all the sessions of the meeting, we had a chance to observe our elders in action and to size them up.

Months before in America I had been given an apt thumbnail sketch of each of my future colleagues by Dr. Zwemer, who was on furlough. Of John Van Ess he said,

"He has a parrot that swears, he is very independent and spends most of his time among the Arab tribes in the desert and marshes, and he has a superb command of Arabic." And then he added casually,

"I don't think you would be at all interested in him."

When I first saw this tall young man in Bahrain, he had a full beard a la Russe, ruddy enough so that he used to refer to it fondly in later years as "Sunrise on the Desert." He smoked more cigarettes than were considered good for him and he had a habit of frowning when intent. This was really because his glasses needed correcting when and if he could get to an oculist, but it gave him a somewhat forbidding appearance.

During that first week he was busy on the language committee conducting examinations for young missionaries; or doing accounts; or preparing the Arabic sermon which he was to deliver on Sunday (and which one of my seniors whispered to me was one of the finest she had ever heard).

The prediction that I wouldn't be interested in him worked both ways, for he certainly didn't show any evidence of the slightest interest in me. A more determined bachelor I have never seen.

The Arabs say "It is written," and so the recalcitrant donkey

on the picnic proved to be the instrument of fate. He slid me
off his back onto the sand squarely at the feet of John Van Ess.
The cool and detached young man who had taken no notice of
me whatever for a week kindly helped me up and dusted me off
and our lifelong association was begun.

During the second week of that fateful mission meeting,
every afternoon after tea four young people went off to walk in
the desert. Christine's partner was Dr. Arthur Bennett, a brilliant surgeon who was John's medical colleague in Basrah and
his greatest friend. On the last day just before the departure of
those who were leaving, John eluded the authorities and secured
me for one last walk. Arthur was not so fortunate, for as he was
looking for Christine, James Moerdyk, the Mission Treasurer,
laid a firm hand on him and marched him off to count out two
thousand silver rupees, and do them up in packets of twenty.
Arthur was inwardly rebellious but outwardly docile—no one
ever dared disobey Jim Moerdyk. The rest of his "courting" had
to be carried on by mail.

How beneficial it was for me to settle down, after those
eventful two weeks, to a stiff program of language work. The
discipline of Arabic study was just what I needed after the
emotional upheaval of my whirlwind courtship. John made it
quite clear to me that he was going to marry me when he
returned from furlough and departed cheerfully leaving me on
my desert island to console myself with Arabic verbs.

We had been very circumspect during the days while we were
getting to know each other and fondly imagined that no one
had noticed us. My language teacher, a Christian Arab from the
north, would sometimes say in the course of a conversation
lesson with elaborate unconcern,

"Did you have a letter from Basrah by the mail boat today?"
A mere exercise in grammar of course. To which I would reply
carefully, in the same spirit,

"No, I did not have a letter from Basrah, but I had one from
Muscat."

He would also run over the pros and cons of foreigners trying
to learn Arabic, and usually wound up by remarking, in a
detached way, that of all our mission no one had mastered
Arabic like Mr. Van Ess.

"None of the rest of you will ever speak it as well as he
does," he would remark lugubriously.

In the face of this discouraging forecast I plodded on with

my Arabic studies in my pedestrian way. Christine and I had a pleasant little home of our own as did the Calverleys, and were gaining useful experience in the mysteries of housekeeping. We all chafed under the sense of uselessness which every language student feels, but we knew that our main business was to learn Arabic. Christine and I had the added incentive of wanting to be qualified before we married our prospective husbands.

In April John stopped in Bahrain for a week on his way to Bombay, enroute to America for his first furlough. We made our engagement public, and received a hearty blessing from all our colleagues.

My mother had been horrified at the speed of my capitulation, and from far-off Chicago had written me a sound scolding for taking up with the first man I met after reaching foreign shores. But as soon as he walked breezily up her front steps and entered the family circle, she took him to her heart.

She was completely satisfied with the result of the meeting on the sand.

II
Son of the Prairies

John Van Ess was born in the pinewoods of Michigan, August 10, 1879, the fourth child of a country clergyman. His father, the Reverend Balster Van Ess, had come as a young adult from the "old country," the Netherlands, where he was born and brought up. His family lived in the province of Groningen, and their son, Balster, received his education at the University of Groningen. When he finished his divinity course and obtained his degree, he decided to do what many of his fellow Dutchmen were doing, and go to America. He felt that opportunities were greater there for a young man.

There were large groups of Hollanders settled in Michigan and Illinois, and young "Dominie Van Ess" had no trouble in establishing himself. His first necessity was to secure his license to be a preacher and pastor in America. He was asked whether he would prefer to take his theological examinations in English or in Latin, and he chose Latin!

The next step was to find himself a wife. He had made friends in South Holland, a country town south of Chicago, whose broad flat fields were ideal for market gardens. The region must have reminded these transplanted Dutchmen very vividly of their sea-level homeland. This rich farming country was then populated almost entirely by families from the Netherlands who prospered exceedingly well. One of the homesteads set amidst its broad acres was that of the Ravesloot family, and here the young clergyman came and wooed and won their daughter Jane.

The youthful minister and his bride went to a pastorate in North Holland, Michigan, a little town not far from the city of Holland. Holland has always been a center for Americans of Dutch birth or ancestry, and today is nationally famous for "Tulip Time" every spring. In the eighteen seventies North Holland was to all intents and purposes a Dutch village. John's mother spoke no English, and he heard very little until his schooldays. Church services were entirely in Dutch.

While the family was still living in Michigan, John's older brother Jacob reached school age. He had a straw hat which he disliked, and one autumn morning instead of going to school, he hid up in the haymow in the barn. The Dominie sensed that his son was playing hookey and went to the barn to look for him. Small John was playing on the floor of the barn, and when his father said to him sternly in Dutch, "Johannes, where is your brother?" he answered untruthfully but loyally, "I don't know." At this point Jacob poked his head out of the haymow and was discovered. The minister hauled him out, jammed his hat on his head and marched him off to school, where he thrashed him in front of his fellow pupils. Then young Mr. Van Ess went home and thrashed little John in his turn, for telling a lie. This part of the incident seemed a little unfair to me when I first heard it, and I have always felt a little inclined to lay it up against my brother-in-law!

When John was four years old his mother died. His oldest sister was a tom-boy, and she has told me she could well remember wearing a long black crepe veil and tearing it on a barbed wire fence on her grandfather's farm. The little boys had crepe bands around their hats on their train journey to the funeral. A memorial booklet was published in Dutch, each page black-bordered, and contained her biography and a description of her funeral, in which five clergymen took part. It extolled her devotion to her faith, her church, and her family, and included a heartfelt tribute from her bereaved husband.

Soon after this, the family moved to Chicago. The Reverend Balster Van Ess was called to a large Dutch church, the First Reformed Church of Roseland, where he remained for the rest of his life. This brought the children close to the wide circle of their mother's relatives in South Holland, and under the stern eye of their maternal grandfather, Johannes Ravesloot. This redoubtable *Grootvader* was a real patriarch, feared and respected and loved by his whole tribe. John was his namesake (he was christened Johannes) and was a special favorite of the old autocrat.

In due course, Dominie Van Ess married again. The children's new mother was a widow with one son, and they became a happy and closeknit family. She was a wonderful person, equally gifted as a housewife and a *Juffrouw* (a term of honor, applied in America to the minister's wife). A woman of grace and distinction, she provided her family with a secure and well-ordered home life. With her own boy and her two stepsons, the two Van Ess girls and a foster sister, she had six lively children to bring up. She and the girls did all the housework of the large parsonage, with guests continually coming and going. I have often heard of the huge layer cakes she baked every Saturday, to serve with coffee on Sunday afternoon to the wives of the elders and deacons. The worthy ladies came to the parsonage for rest and refreshment after the afternoon service, while their husbands—the "Greater Consistory"—had their weekly meeting with the Dominie. The house had to be spic and span from garret to cellar to pass the inspection of these sharp-eyed and critical Dutch housewives.

The coffeepot was always on the stove in every Dutch home, and children as well as grownups drank coffee at all hours. I was horrified when I was first married, to see small children with large cups in front of them—I was allowed to drink neither tea nor coffee till I was twenty! John assured me that he had his first coffee when he was a few hours old, lying across the lap of the midwife who had brought him into the world. She gave him a few drops from the spoon of her own cup, and he smacked his lips, and as he said gaily to me,

"I have been drinking coffee ever since!"

John's step-brother, William Van Kersen, was a little older than he. No blood brothers could have been more devoted to each other than these two were throughout their lives. Curiously enough, they were the two members of the family who were considered to look alike, though they were not related in any way. Will became an official in the Board of Foreign Missions of the Reformed Church, and in the late 1920's went to all the mission fields with a deputation. He entered Iraq by way of Mosul and Baghdad, and was hailed in both these cities by Arabs, who said to him in Arabic,

"Greetings, Mr. Van Ess! When did you arrive here from Basrah?" Dr. Mylrea of the Mission, who was accompanying the party from America, and acting as their interpreter, would explain and the invariable comment was,

"We should know you are his brother, because you look just like him!"

John's father was a remarkable man, and made a distinguished record in the large church which he so ably led. Over the years, in widely scattered Reformed churches across America, I have had people exclaim to me when they heard my name,

"Your husband's father was the best preacher I have ever heard!"

At the time of his death, two of his sons were students at

Princeton Theological Seminary. They divided his sermon sketches between them, and when they returned to their studies, John presented one of his father's outlines in a class on sermon-making. It was duly discussed in class and the professor eyed his student very sharply. After class, John went up as he had always intended to do, to explain the experiment to his teacher, but before he had time to do so, the professor exclaimed,

"Young man, that was a very remarkable sermon outline! It was much too mature to be the work of a theological student without experience!"

The elder Van Ess was as gifted a pastor as he was preacher. "Ask the Dominie!" was the cry throughout his large parish, whether it was for advice about business, marriage, or spiritual difficulties. Some families would not take medicine prescribed by the doctor until the minister had given his approval. When he went and spent a summer in the Netherlands, all the christenings were saved up till his return, and the line of babies in parents' arms stretched across the front of the church several times.

The stately music of the glorious Dutch Psalms, and the beautiful Reformed Church liturgy, made all the church services memorable. A feature of church attendance which the Van Ess children remembered all their lives, was the passing down the line in a pew, of the *ruik dosje* when the small fry became restless or sleepy. This was a little silver box, with a compartment at each end. One held peppermints and the other a piece of sponge soaked in Eau de Cologne. Refreshed by these, the youngsters could endure the rest of the long service with comparative patience.

The children attended the Chicago public schools, as their father wanted them to be good Americans. With that established, he encouraged them to take pride in their Dutch heritage, and to realize how much the little nation of their forebears had contributed to the great new country.

They were made free on the prairies which still surrounded the country towns in that part of Illinois. John loved the wide horizons and the vast open spaces, and as long as he lived he preferred level country to mountains or hills. The boys learned early to skate and to swim.

They were as much at home in the church as in the parsonage. Once a group of inspectors from a fire insurance com-

pany were looking over the church premises, and inquired if
there was any way of getting up into the top of the tower.

"I don't know of any," answered a member of the church
committee who was with them.

"I do!" volunteered a leggy half grown boy who was hovering
around; and the minister's youngest son showed them the
somewhat tortuous route to the upper part of the tower,
familiar to him from his explorations.

When he was in college, John's fondness for exploits in
towers nearly caused him to be expelled on several occasions.
Once he and some friends tried to steal the clapper from the
bell that called them to classes; another time they maneuvered a
surprised and unwilling cow all the way up into the belfry.

He and his brothers all attended preparatory school and later
Hope College, in Holland, Michigan, which has always been a
cultural and educational center for Americans of Dutch background. The rules were strict in those days and John was often
in hot water with the authorities for other reasons than tower-
climbing. He was high spirited and mischievous, but an excellent
student and made a fine scholastic record. He seriously considered studying law after college: he had a keen analytical
mind and was deeply interested in politics. However, he decided
that he was still more interested in Semitic languages, and went
to Princeton, New Jersey, to the Theological Seminary, where
the professors were outstanding. Both his brother Jacob and his
step-brother Will Van Kersen were students there, preparing for
the ministry.

Here he distinguished himself in both Hebrew and Arabic,
and became absorbed in original textual research in the Old
Testament under one of the foremost of his professors, Robert
Dick Wilson. An academic career seemed a foregone conclusion.
But just at the psychological moment, an appeal was made for a
young man to replace a gifted recruit to the Arabian Mission
who had died of smallpox soon after reaching the field. John
had known him and admired his dedication. Here was a chance
to meet the Arabs on their own ground, instead of through
grammars and dictionaries. The call was irresistible and he
answered it. In 1902, at the age of twenty-three, John Van Ess
went out to begin his life-long career in the Arab world.

III

Daughter of New England

I was born and brought up in a quiet country town north of Boston, which had been my mother's birthplace before me, and where she had always lived. Wakefield changed far less between her childhood and mine than it has done since. Like her, I attended the "North Ward School," an old-fashioned district school with six grades in one room, taught by one long-suffering teacher. There was a huge stove in one corner, with a woodbox beside it, and in the entry where we hung our coats, and the country children their dinner pails, a big bucket of drinking water with a shiny tin dipper floating in it.

In winter I slid down the long snowy hills on my father's sled, a relic of his boyhood in Vermont. After I was grown-up I asked my mother if she knew that I used to coast down Salem Street Hill when I was a little girl. This was a wonderful hill for sliding, but it ended at the bottom on a grade crossing of the railroad track and was very dangerous. She said,

"Yes, I thought you probably did, because I did when I was a child, although my mother had forbidden it. I didn't want you to disobey me, so I didn't tell you not to!"

We lived beside one of New England's loveliest small lakes, and in winter when the ice was hard my father used to skate across it to the railway station every morning. He would leave his skates there and board the train for Boston. One of my most vivid childhood memories is of standing in the window-seat of our sitting room with my mother beside me, a baby in her arms, waving goodbye to my father as he skimmed over the ice till he was out of sight. Today Route 128 goes on the other side of that well-loved lake, and my grandchildren are thrilled to have me point it out and say, "There is the place where your great-grandfather skated on his way to business."

Lake Quannapowitt was also a famous center for ice-boat races—a thrilling and dangerous sport which it was good fun to watch. The great white sails were like huge birds, and the sharp runners cut over the smooth ice with incredible speed.

Another delightful and hazardous pastime for us children in

winter was to hitch our sleds on to the back of delivery wagons on runners, called "pungs," and to go bumping and jolting along the hard-packed snowy roads when the horse began to run.

In summer there were sailboats of every size and kind on our lake, and amateur regattas were often held. We children were supposed never to go out in rowboats without a grownup, but when I was about twelve, I took a younger cousin for a venturesome voyage on a large raft. We got much farther out in the lake than I intended, and it was a tense moment when I discovered that my pole wouldn't touch the bottom. However, I managed to negotiate the raft safely to shore, and when I was soundly scolded by both our mothers (and no doubt punished) I replied grandly,

"I know every drop of water in this lake!"

My Pilgrim ancestry, on my mother's side, was so familiar to me that I took it for granted. We visited cousins in Duxbury and on Cape Cod (always known as The Cape) and I used to compare their ship models, and the fascinating little boats in bottles, with the large paintings in our house of my grandfather's clipper ships. He had run away to sea when he was nine years old, and was a sea-faring man all his life. My grandmother made two voyages around the world with him in a sailing ship—a proof of deep devotion, as she wasn't a good sailor.

My Aunt Dora, my mother's only sister, had a strong sense of history, and she took me to all the famous places in our vicinity: Plymouth, Concord and Lexington, Salem, and all over Boston. She included the literary shrines as well, and the beautiful Longfellow house in Cambridge, the House of Seven Gables in Salem, Whittier's tranquil birthplace in Haverhill, and Emerson's classic home in Concord, with the near-by Alcott home of the cherished "Little Women," became part of my childhood background.

I loved it all except for one unfortunate association with the Washington Elm in Cambridge (now regrettably gone). I hated arithmetic and was never any good at it, and I well recall sitting at my school desk with my tears falling on my slate, washing out one unsuccessful attempt after another to compute the area of all the leaves on the Washington Elm.

A few years later I became familiar with my father's Vermont origins, when we began as a family to spend our summers there. He was born in Huntington Center, on the slopes of Camel's

Hump, and he spent his early boyhood in Richmond, on the Winooski River. His father kept the country store and was a member of the State Legislature in Montpelier.

We used to stay in a charming old red brick farmhouse, the home of one of my father's boyhood friends, and drive about in the glorious Green Mountain country, covering as great a radius as a pair of stout farm horses could achieve in a day. We became familiar with all my father's early haunts, and took especial pride in a wooded knoll still called "Firman Hill," which was probably part of the original grant of land to the Firman who came from Connecticut and settled in Vermont in the late eighteenth century. My father knew that he came of good pioneer stock, but he had no interest whatever in ancestors. It was not until recent years (and this through the interest and research of my sister's husband, Lennig Sweet) that I have discovered that the first Firman to come to the New World was only ten years later than my mother's forebears on the Mayflower. John Firman sailed to America from Ipswich in 1630, with what was known as the Winthrop Fleet. (And what fun I had a few years ago in England, going to the little Suffolk village of Nayland, and finding in the parish church register the record of births, deaths and marriages of long ago "ffyrmyns.")

Two experiences of early childhood influenced my whole later life. One was the first nurse I ever had, a young Negro girl called Lavinia Bess. She came up from Hampton Institute in Virginia, where my aunt taught, to help my youthful mother. She sang me Negro spirituals long before they were generally known or appreciated, and gave me warm and loving companionship which evoked deep affection from me. Association with her conditioned me to feel that affection and sympathy for her race all the rest of my life.

The other experience was meeting the great pioneer missionary Cyrus Hamlin, who founded Robert College in Constantinople (now Istanbul) in Turkey. When he had first gone to the Near East he travelled by a sailing ship on which my grandfather was a young officer, and they became great friends. As long as Dr. Hamlin lived, he used to come once a year to Wakefield to call on the widow of his old friend. How clearly I remember sitting on a little stool (we called it a "cricket") beside my grandmother's rocking chair, looking up with awe at a tall old gentleman with white side whiskers.

"This is Dr. Cyrus Hamlin of Turkey," she said proudly to me. I am sure that the strong attraction the Near East has always held for me dated from that time.

When I was twelve years old, my father's business took him to Chicago, and my happy New England childhood was over. This was a tremendous uprooting, especially for my mother and me. My father was forward looking and completely absorbed in the present and the future, and my brother and sister were very small, but mother and I mourned for our New England home. She learned to love Chicago much sooner than I did, and speedily identified herself with many activities in that bustling, new, midwest city.

My father was a highly gifted businessman, and advanced rapidly in the firm of Marshall Field and Company in Chicago, becoming one of its top executives before his early death in 1911. Along with his business genius, he had a strong sense of Christian stewardship, and of deep dedication to every cause which helped the underprivileged. He lavished time and money on city missions, and on home and foreign work: missionary, benevolent, and humanitarian. My mother shared his interests to the full and had the same gifts of leadership. For years she was the head of a nation-wide missionary organization of Congregational women, and she spent the last years of her active life in a Christian settlement house in the slums of Chicago. Here she was a near neighbor of Jane Addams of Hull House; they became good friends and often worked closely together.

The city mission church, around which developed later this Christian social center, was the one of my father's many projects in which we all shared as a family. Every Sunday afternoon, after a hurried lunch (referred to by one of our friends as "Firman's consecrated hash") we all drove in a roomy "carry-all," drawn by a horse, to what was then Ewing Street Church, just off Halsted Street, in time for Sunday school. In summer we were provided by friends with a bouquet for each person present at the service and we looked like a florist's van. We learned to know every individual, helped with the many summer picnics when different groups came out to our spacious home and lovely grounds in Oak Park, and shared in all the celebrations at Christmas and other special times throughout the year.

My father was a great believer in having children learn Scripture by heart, and he used to offer prizes to these little city dwellers when they could repeat Psalms and other Bible passages without a mistake. This practice began with his own family (but without prizes!) and we always repeated Psalms or other Scripture passages at our family prayers at breakfast. We children memorized easily, but when my father gave us the twelfth chapter of Ecclesiastes ("Remember now thy Creator in the days of thy youth") the younger ones found it difficult. My brother Royal was eight or nine then, and my mother privately promised him a dollar if he would have it letter perfect by Saturday night. My father found her out and was justly indignant.

"I won't have my children bribed to learn the Bible!" he reproached her.

"It isn't a bribe, it's a reward," was her spirited reply. "And anyhow, it is much better than being made to learn Bible passages as a punishment, as I had to when I was a child!"

I don't remember how it came out, but I am sure my brother got his dollar.

My father was a loving and often indulgent parent, but he was very strict. As I was growing up, dancing, cards, and the theatre were forbidden and Sabbath keeping was rigid. I couldn't have cared less about dancing, as I didn't like boys and never had dates, and cards meant nothing to me then; but I did regret not being allowed to go to the theatre. However, we went to many excellent concerts and lectures and always had a box at Orchestra Hall at Christmas time, when the Thomas Orchestra and the Apollo Club gave "The Messiah."

One thing under which I did groan was my father's insistence on saying a blessing before meals in hotels and on dining cars when we were travelling, and having family prayers in our "sections" in the sleeping car.

"But Papa," I would protest, "people will notice us and think that we are peculiar."

"Let them notice us," was his reply. "It would be a good thing if more people followed our example."

I made up my mind then that when I had children of my own I would never subject them to this embarrassment, and I never did, but sometimes I wonder if I was wrong.

I have often wondered, too, how my father would have reacted if he had lived long enough to see my brother and sister grow up. Royal and Helen were much gayer and more socially inclined than I had been, and my mother relaxed many of the prohibitions which had been imposed on me. On my first furlough I protested to her about something they did on Sunday which I considered unsuitable.

"Papa wouldn't have liked it!" I exclaimed indignantly.

"My dear child," she replied comfortingly, "if your father had lived he would have had to adjust his attitude about many things. As you grow older you may keep your own convictions but you must learn to be tolerant to other points of view and accept the fact that times change."

I am sure that she was right, for my father had a strong sense of justice, and a wide experience in dealing with all sorts and conditions of people.

Our home was the center for every kind of hospitality—rich and poor, old and young, informal and formal: guests for one meal or visitors for months. At our very large and assorted Thanksgiving parties, Papa used to entertain the company after dinner, when they were full of turkey and pumpkin pie, by standing on his head for several minutes at a time—an accomplishment for which he was justly famous. He would offer any of the men guests a handsome present for their pet charity if they could do the same, but I don't think anyone ever did. He was very athletic and kept himself in excellent condition by horse-back riding every morning before breakfast and by tennis, bowling, and regular exercises.

While I was in college my father used to come to see me whenever a business trip took him back to Massachusetts and he would "blow in" with boxes of Page and Shaw candy for me and my friends and take me out for a drive. In winter he would get a sleigh and a fast horse at the village livery stable, bid me bundle up warmly, and off we would speed over the snowy New England hills. After one of these excursions I was doing my hour of "domestic work" in the dormitory pantry before dinner and one of the Irish maids said to me admiringly,

"Who was the swell looking fellow I saw you out with this afternoon, Miss Firman?"

"My father!" I replied proudly.

"Aw, go on wid' ye' " she said incredulously.

He was only twenty four years old when I was born and kept his youthful looks all his life. There was a very close bond between us, and his death in 1911, just before I was married (when he was only forty-nine), was the most overwhelming blow I had ever experienced.

My college years were very happy ones; after four years in a midwest high school, excellent as it was, I rejoiced to return to my beloved New England. The somewhat austere atmosphere of Mount Holyoke College in those days, under the wise and enlightened leadership of President Mary E. Woolley, was very congenial to me; so was the intellectual discipline and the inspiration of notable professors.

I received my B.A. in 1906 and went on to Wellesley to work for my Master's degree in English Literature under the direction of the incomparable Katherine Lee Bates of "America the Beautiful" fame. This achieved I went to my first and only teaching job in America, to Carleton College in Northfield, Minnesota as a very young Instructor in English Literature.

The atmosphere of the college was delightful, the faculty congenial, and my students—some of them older than I was—were responsive and on the whole rewarding. I fully intended to continue there for some years and then go East again, or to England, and work for my Ph.D. in one of the large universities. The scholar's life had made a strong appeal to me while I was working for my Master's degree, and I had deep admiration for the great women on the Mount Holyoke and Wellesley faculties who combined scholarship and teaching.

As the year went on I began to feel misgivings. These nice people were all so secure, so comfortable and so privileged. I couldn't forget the people I had known in the poor districts of Chicago, when I had worked there on my vacations for some of the many welfare organizations in which my parents were active. Their deep concern for the underprivileged had undoubtedly "rubbed off" on me.

I wrote to my father and told him how I felt and asked him what he would think of my leaving Carleton after that year and going to Chicago Commons to train as a social worker. He replied, very sensibly, that I had had a long and expensive education to become a teacher, that I was extremely lucky to have such a good job when I was young and inexperienced, and that his opinion was that I should continue for the present in what I had begun. I recognized the logic of his answer and accepted his decision.

At this psychological moment, Providence intervened. Sitting one morning at college chapel, in a long row with my fellow faculty members on the platform, I settled myself to listen politely to the speaker of the day. He was Dr. Samuel Zwemer of the Student Volunteer Movement and one of the founders of the Arabian Mission of the Reformed Church in America. He gave a graphic description of the whole peninsula of Arabia and his extensive travels there; a vivid sketch of the mission stations and their activities; and concluded with a spirited appeal for a young woman teacher to go to Basrah (in what was then Turkish Arabia) to open a school for Arab girls.

Like a flash of lightning the conviction came to me "This means me."

Some people experience instant conversion. I never did because my whole environment, home, school, and church, fostered a steady and gradual growth in the life of the spirit. Some people fall in love at first sight. I didn't, it took me two weeks. But the "call" to my life work came to me in a split second. The whole pattern of my life fell into place.

The spark of interest in the Near East kindled so long ago, burst into a steady flame. I had long had a deep romantic interest in the mysterious and secluded life of Muslim women; I read Pierre Loti's *Disenchanted* and Hichens' *Garden of Allah*, and other equally unrealistic but enthralling pictures of the Muslim East, as well as more authentic descriptions. Now came the opportunity to invade that seclusion with modern education, and it was an inspiration and a challenge.

My parents approved, my credentials were satisfactory, and I was duly appointed to the Arabian Mission. Buoyantly I told my college friends that I was going out to establish the Mount Holyoke of the Persian Gulf.

Full of idealism and hope, and in sublime ignorance of what lay before me, I set out to the Arab world to fulfil my destiny.

IV
The Missionary Vocation

"Deep in the heart of each member of the Arabian Mission has always been a sense of imperativeness to the point of thralldom and yet with it a sense of emancipation that comes with the consciousness of being held by an irresistible and ultimately triumphant idea."

So said my husband, John Van Ess, many years after the founding of the Arabian Mission of the Reformed Church in America. It had been founded because of the burning conviction of one man that the Gospel should be carried to Muslims in their homeland of Arabia. That man was Dr. John G. Lansing, a professor in the New Brunswick Theological Seminary, and the idea of attempting this seemingly impossible task became an obsession with him.

John Van Ess continued:

For sheer effrontery the idea was unsurpassed for in that homeland was entrenched the greatest adversary* of Christ and His message. The adversary was entrenched behind a simple but unyielding creed. He was surrounded physically by trackless deserts and historically by a reputation for invincibility. The path to his mind and heart was guarded by an appallingly difficult language.

The idea caught the imagination of Samuel Zwemer and James Cantine, who were students in the Seminary, and on completion of their studies they went to Arabia. They were followed by others: clergymen, doctors, nurses and teachers; both men and women. The powers of darkness, sensing an invasion, smote the invaders in body, soul, and mind—in body with sickness, in soul with temptation, in mind with doubt. But steadily their numbers grew. The Church at home, fascinated by the spectacle of her sons and daughters attempting the impossible, prayed and gave and encouraged. Stone by stone, brick by brick, schools and hospitals and houses arose. Again and again

*Cf. p. 34

the enemy struck, sometimes with death. He seemed to prefer the first-born. Yet always, through shimmering noondays and through choking nights, centers of work were established from which went out the missionary effort and influence.

The words imperativeness, thralldom, and emancipation lie at the heart of the missionary vocation. The missionary is under orders, subject to the command: "Go ye into all the world and preach the Gospel to every creature." "Gospel" means Good News. To one person the assurance of personal immortality would be the best possible news; to another the promise of a rich and satisfying life in this world. Others would see the prospect of alleviating suffering and wrongs as the most welcome expectation.

Our motivation as missionaries is basically to put ourselves in harmony with God and with His purposes for the universe. This is achieved by obeying the command to go into all the world and preach the Gospel and to show the relationship of man to God expressed in Christian service.

Christian humanitarianism is a result of this attitude of heart and mind but it is not the motive itself. Christ said to Peter, "Feed my sheep," and this is certainly carried out in medical work, in relief and rehabilitation, and in educating the ignorant and giving them the means to make their lives more abundant both physically and spiritually.

Another aspect is to preach salvation—the old fashioned expression was "to save souls from Hell." A more acceptable phrasing to most people today is that salvation is to attain healing, wholeness and completeness. The broken relationship between man and God is restored and a complete reconciliation is achieved.

Establishing the Church all over the world has been the aim of missionary work, Roman Catholic and Protestant alike, throughout the centuries. Many of the "splinter groups" now operating energetically in most non-Christian countries attempt to do this for their own particular brand of theology. It is unfortunate that they are often condemnatory of all other Christian bodies and that the confusion resulting from missionary multiplicity has an adverse effect on the whole cause. The Ecumenical Movement stresses the great essential truths in which all Christians believe.

Oil companies pay large salaries to their staffs in difficult climates and offer generous "fringe benefits." The United States Government gives special allowances to Foreign Service personnel in hardship posts. Often the transplanted families make little sealed American or English communities and live in them completely insulated from the foreign world outside.

Missionaries learn the language and try to live as close to the people of their adopted country as they can. The missionary is sustained by his profound sense of commitment which is the first essential for all persons who have experienced an authentic call to Christian service in a foreign country. The Apostle Paul says:

"If the trumpet give an uncertain sound, who shall prepare himself to the battle?"

A deep conviction is the only thing that can carry one safely through the hardships, frustrations and disillusionments of missionary life. Career perspective sets it in relation to all of time, not just the present moment, and material standards take a second place. A tourist in the Far East was watching a nun who belonged to a nursing order give an injection to a particularly repulsive leper. Overcome with horror and revulsion he exclaimed,

"I wouldn't do that for a million dollars!"

"Neither would I," answered the nun quietly.

In 1906 John attended a conference in Cairo and presented a paper, in the course of a series on Methods of Mission Work among Muslims, called "Converts and Backsliders." His conclusion was as follows:

Finally, our aim is to make converts and to that end we stretch all our energies and spend our money. But is that really our aim? Suppose now that we have the convert, does our endeavor stop there? Suppose the whole world were converted, is that our goal?

Our duty, rather our whole work, only begins there. As the mechanic who by patient toil has repaired and made anew the broken parts of his machine, but whose eye and heart are all the time set on the moment when he can draw back the lever and let the mighty steam into the waiting parts; so patiently, prayerfully and persistently we try to set God's world right. Only then, however, is our task really beginning. With Christ high in the steam-gauge and willing hands and hearts and heads the Christian Catholic Church shall begin to render to God triune the praise so long His due.

Our aim then is not converts, not churches, not schools, but harmony—harmony with God and communion with Him.

The occasions which crystallize these motives so that they are made concrete in action are many and varied. Late in life John wrote:

My interest in the Arabs began when I started to study their language at Princeton. It has all the dignity of Latin, the variety of English, the beauty of Italian, the sonority of German, the flexibility of Greek and the bewilderment of Russian.

In my own case it was the specific challenge of one particular job which brought all my vague aspirations into focus and gave me a clear call.

Whatever the motive or mixture of motives that impels people to become missionaries, the result is that they achieve an inner fulfillment which satisfies deep spiritual needs.

The qualifications of missionary candidates are thoroughly investigated before they are considered for service overseas. A prospective missionary must be trained to a profession: teaching, medicine, evangelism, social work, or other specialized skills. He must be capable of learning a difficult foreign language. His health must be good. He must be adaptable: physically, mentally and spiritually.

Most important of all is to possess what anthropologists call cultural empathy. This is indispensable for success in missionary life. To be at home in the world of Arab men and women and to be accepted there was one of the richest experiences of our lives.

This isn't just a matter of knowing the correct salutations, or always using your right hand in giving something to another person, or not turning the sole of your foot to anyone. These are details and they are important but the supreme fact is the rapport between yourself and your Arab friends, and the recognition of the worth of personality.

This was in line with John's experience when he was invited to a memorial service for King Feisal the First in a mosque in

Zobeir. He found that he was the only non-Muslim there and when he expressed surprise was told,

"It is just because you are a missionary and are true to the tenets of your faith as you understand them that we trust you. As the Arab proverb has it, 'He who is true to Allah will not betray Abdullah.' "

They even asked him to make a speech but he declined for reasons of expediency.

I have always remembered an incident of my own early years when I was going for the first time to a large Muslim religious ceremony for women. The friend who invited me was a mullaya, a woman religious leader, and she and I had agreed that I should go in Arab dress so as to be inconspicuous. When I got to her house ready to put on the "nice clean set of clothes" she had promised me she had changed her mind.

"You would violate your personality," she said, "if you put on Arab clothes. Everyone knows that you are an American and a Christian and they respect you because you live up to your religious beliefs. You must be yourself."

As soon as new missionaries arrive on the field they begin a rigorous course of preparation. Our mission requires two years of language study with examinations at the end of each year. Besides this intensive study of the Arabic language we have a course on Islamics and on the history and culture of Arab countries. It was a shock to me when I first realized that Muslims, devoted followers of the great monotheistic ideology of Islam, consider the Christian doctrine of the Trinity to be blasphemy. Their creed is contained in their "Witness": "There is no God but God and Mohammed is the apostle of God." The other of the Five Pillars of their religion are prayer, fasting, almsgiving, and the pilgrimage to Mecca.

A knowledge of the politics of the Muslim countries is also essential. A King, a Sultan, a Sheikh, has to be recognized in just the right way. The sensitive highly nationalistic governments emerging all over the world today have to be understood and deferred to if one is to be tolerated within their borders. Tribal loyalties and enmities were of great importance in the early decades of our mission.

The classic methods of missionary work are preaching, teaching, and healing. For several generations the "Muslim Controversy" was widely used. Christian theologians pitted their wits against superbly trained Muslim ecclesiastics in debates which were intellectual exercises of the highest order. Today the opposite approach is employed and the great religious truths common to both Christianity and Islam are the foundation for discussions. Kenneth Cragg's *The Call of the Minaret* and *Sandals at the Mosque* analyze and inform in the light of this standpoint. The Muslim is no longer considered an enemy but a worshipper of God whom he conceives as Allah.

Preachers today stress the great affirmations of Christianity. Visual aids, literature, discussion groups in well stocked bookshops, and varied contacts are used. Touring was the backbone of our mission work for many years. In the early days when no doctors had permanently joined the mission the intrepid young clergymen would set off with a bag full of Arabic Bibles and Christian literature, a set of dental tools, and a supply of what they referred to as "harmless but effective remedies." They had taken First Aid courses and they doctored everything from colic to cholera. Fortunately they never killed anyone as far as I know.

Before my husband left America the first time he was given by a dentist friend a set of instruments and a brief course of instruction. This somewhat off-beat technical skill stood him in good stead on many occasions. Years ago when he was on the Pirate Coast (now known as the Trucial Coast) he was holding an informal clinic and a big Negress was brought to him with a roaring toothache. She wanted the tooth pulled and he had a terrible time getting it out. He said,

"I practically had to put my knee on the woman's chest, and when the tooth finally came out, I was sure I must have broken her jaw."

However his patient wiped her face on the corner of her veil and pointed inside saying,

"Here's another!"

Teaching has been one of the greatest contributions made by missions. From large universities with graduate and technical schools, high schools and grammar schools, down to the simplest group of village children learning their alphabets, the minds and hearts of millions have been influenced in their formative years all over the world.

My husband's greatest asset professionally was his mastery of Arabic. He wrote several of his own text books in Arabic which are still in use in the boys' school in Basrah. He also developed a series of reading charts for beginners in Arabic, graphically illustrated, which all the primary classes in the school used with great success. These, although done independently, were similar in principle to the Laubach Literacy Charts now used in many languages.

In the pioneer days of the generation to which John and I belonged we needed all the organizing ability we possessed to carry out our work in the framework of our environment.

This was especially true for our medical workers. Our colleague, Dr. Paul Harrison, was a distinguished surgeon and was made a Fellow of the American Society of Surgeons for a new technique he evolved for hernia operations and for experiments with spinal anesthesia. It was said of him in the early days that he operated most brilliantly if the patient was lying on a kitchen table in a dark room in an Arab house and a helper was holding up a hurricane lantern to give him a little more light.

Cornelia Dalenberg, a nurse, used to deliver babies in Ma'adan huts in the river country of Iraq; I went with her once to see a pair of twins whom she had brought into the world the day before and the only entrance to the hut was so low that we had to bend almost double to get in.

Today all our hospitals have the most modern equipment but when making outcalls or touring our doctors and nurses are still obliged to do their work under very primitive conditions. Perhaps the greatest single boon in our hospitals now is air conditioning. Formerly when a surgeon was operating in summer one of his staff had to stand beside him to keep wiping off the perspiration with a Turkish towel.

Members of our mission developed special skills. Two clergymen, Dirk Dykstra and Garrett De Jong, were outstanding as architects and builders, using materials available and training local workmen. Some of the techniques they evolved and architectural features which they introduced have been extensively followed and are in general use today.

Josephine Van Peursem learned Braille in English and then in Arabic when she became responsible for an orphanage which included a number of blind children. Other pupils came to her when they heard of this marvellous opportunity and a wide circle of sightless people were helped to independent living.

Every skill and every aptitude and every gift of personality is used to the utmost capacity in the missionary vocation.

V

Solo in Desert and Marshes

When the young man from the prairies of America reached the deserts of Arabia, he found himself one of a group of youthful, energetic pioneers in an entirely new field. Older missions in the Near East, in Egypt, Syria, Turkey, and Persia, had begun working with members of the Oriental churches: Orthodox, Armenian, Coptic, Nestorian, Syriac. The Arabian Mission intended to work directly with Muslim Arabs.

Basrah, the station to which John was assigned, was then (1902) part of the Turkish Empire. The other mission stations were each under a different government. Bahrain, the little island near to the Arabian shore of the Persian Gulf, was ruled by a Sheikh who had British protection; Muscat, on the Gulf of Oman near the Arabian Sea, was in the Sultanate of Oman. Kuwait had not yet become a station of the mission.

But Basrah, like all the rest of the "Land Between the Two Rivers" which is now Iraq, was also Arab country. Though it was governed by Turkish officials, they were aliens in language and culture, and both tribesmen and town dwellers resented their presence. Anyone who wanted to win the friendship and confidence of the Arabs, in towns or tribes, first and foremost had to have a good knowledge of the Arabic language.

John Van Ess had received a thorough grounding in grammar and reading at Princeton. Now he needed to get out among the Arabs and apply his "book learning" to mastering the spoken word. His bi-lingual heritage no doubt helped him, but he had a natural facility for learning languages, and after a few months in a completely Arab environment he was talking "the language of the angels" as though it were his own.

He came before the language committee of the mission, at the end of his first year, with considerable self assurance. Understandably, this rather nettled his slightly older colleagues, and they were severe and exacting in examining him.

At one point they challenged him on an obscure point in grammar and John hotly disputed it with them; they consulted an authority and found that he was right, but they marked him down fifteen percent anyway for impudence.

These were pioneer days and each person was very much on his own. After concluding his language course and brilliantly passing his final examinations John was given a roving commission based in Basrah. He left civilization often for months at a time and explored thoroughly the marshes and deserts of lower Iraq. For years he used to wring my heart by telling me pathetically that one winter when he was in a far-off Arab encampment in December his Christmas dinner consisted of a plate of rice and a radish. He told it once too often and a great light broke on me.

"You didn't mind at all!" I cried accusingly. "You loved being off among the Arabs by yourself!"

John laughed and admitted cheerfully that he had only been trying to work on my sympathies.

There was a story current (I have always wondered if it was apocryphal) that one of his travel documents was a cancelled insurance policy, impressive with its various seals; and that he or one of his colleagues used Mrs. Worrall's midwifery diploma to impress minor officials as they travelled in Asiatic Turkey.

One of the longest of these early tours, about 1905, was from the Euphrates River through the marshes to the Tigris, crossing a sort of inverted triangle whose base was the Shatt-el-Hai. For many years British river steamers had skirted the Tigris side of this triangle on their way to Baghdad but the Euphrates side was too shallow for steam traffic and only native craft plied its waters.

From Gurna (the traditional site of the garden of Eden) for eighty miles northwest the Euphrates ran into a huge marsh, the channel being marked only by a narrow path through the high reeds. This area was menaced by river pirates, Ma'adan Arabs, who found sailboats an easier prey than the "smoke boat" on the navigable Tigris River. They took a heavy toll in plunder and blood especially in spring when the water was high.

No foreigners—Europeans or Turks—had ever penetrated this country though several unsuccessful attempts had been made, the most recent when a French exploring party had been stopped by Turkish officials. This region was all part of John Van Ess's "parish," as his general assignment was touring. The challenge to venture into unknown and dangerous territory was too tempting for him to resist. He wrote in his report to headquarters:

> With life so short and such a large section entirely on my shoulders and conscience; with high water, cool weather, good health, now if ever was the chance. To prove that an unarmed missionary can go farther than an armed government, I took the chance.

Another reason was to collect data for Sir William Will-cocks, a famous British irrigation engineer who had been investigating the country as far north as Baghdad. He had begun modern irrigation in Egypt and had been asked to draw up a plan for the irrigation of Mesopotamia. John had met him and was later to accompany him on some of his trips. Sir William had suggested that it would be useful to acquire as much preliminary information as possible before undertaking the scientific expedition.

"On the first of May," recounted the young explorer,

we started from Nasiriyeh, our out-station on the Euphrates, where I had been spending a month. The party consisted of a captain, two sailors, myself and a cook—a Syrian Jacobite. The first day up the Shatt-el-Hai was uneventful, along a route well travelled and safe. Unfortunately, owing to a dam, our boat grounded about a mile down the stream. With the sun already low, I did not relish the idea of spending the night in that wild plain, so pushed on afoot to persuade the keepers of the dam to open long enough to give my boat sufficient water to pull up. There were two of them, armed with rifles, and already in an ugly temper owing to two boats of Turks who had been trying for a passage for three hours past. At last, by duly impressing upon them my friendship with the Pasha at Nasiriyeh, and after many a threat and some scuffling, with an oath they broke away a corner of the mud dam. After two hours my boat hove into sight.

At sunrise the dam was entirely demolished, and we proceeded on our way to Shattra, a large and thriving town and a center of trade with the Arabs. At about five in the afternoon we had still about three hours to go, and the raindrops began to fall. Long before sunset the sky was black and a fresh wind was blowing us against the bank, impeding our progress. At nine we reached Shattra but, owing to the wind, could not cross, as the river is wide and deep at this time of the year, and our poles could not touch bottom. So we decided to tie fast until the wind should die down a trifle.

Utterly fatigued, we all soon fell asleep in the boat. At midnight I was awakened by a loud clap of thunder. The wind had veered and was blowing a hurricane and the boat was madly tossing about. From the peculiar motion I could feel that the stern had become loosened and that in a few minutes the bow, too, would give way and we might be driven to the other side—probably to be upset or crushed by collision with the boats on the opposite shore. I called loudly to the captain to get up and tie fast but he was already awake, shivering with fear, and his only reply was to lie whining and calling on Allah for help. On leaving Nasiriyeh a friendly Turk had pressed a 44-calibre Smith-Wesson revolver into my hand. Why I took it I don't know, as it was against my principles, but there it was and at the captain's head. Thus persuaded, he called the sailors and crept out to the shore, lashing the rope firmly around his waist. The wind was howling fiercely, peal on peal of thunder crashed through the sky, the rain fell in torrents, and there in the bow of the boat I crouched, a man of peace, with rain-soaked khakis, keeping the sailors at their posts with a revolver. It was indeed incongruous, and I laughed in the black night for I imagined how I would have looked in an American pulpit in that attitude. And so we waited drearily till morning, when we crossed to Shattra and settled in the khan.

After a few days in Shattra, I broached the subject to the local Turkish governor of crossing the triangle, but was met with blunt refusal. He vowed that four regiments of soldiers could not pass that way, that I would be summarily butchered, and so on. All I might do was to go to Hataman, a small trading post twenty miles inland. For eight hours we followed the devious course of a small stream until it led into a large inland lake, deep at this time of year and fully four miles wide.

Here the Mudir (the head man), a fatherly old Arab, was hospitable but opposed to further travel. He told the young foreigner that the desert was hot and full of hardships, the tribes up in arms; that a light-haired Franjy (the term for all Europeans) even in Arab dress, was too conspicuous, and that he'd better go back the way he came. But I was determined and persistent and finally found a young Arab who agreed to guide me by a roundabout way to the tribe of the Beni Said on the edge of the desert.

It was finally decided to start at the first streaks of dawn. After supper the Mudir kindly took me for a walk in the desert, and then there was a two hour's talk at the door of his hut, while the Arabs gathered and plied me with questions about Frankistan (the general name for all foreign countries). As evidence of our genius in machinery, a Dover egg beater was produced, used by the Mudir for making butter in small quantities. He had just brought it from Baghdad. Amid the exclamations of the bystanders it was pronounced a marvel.

After the guests had departed I tried to sleep, but for a long time would continually start up at the clank of a chain near my head. At first I thought it was a mare tethered at the door, until closer inspection revealed a prisoner firmly shackled by the ankles. Later the Mudir told me he had been too free with his gun and said he tried these measures to impress upon the culprit the advisability of a judicious use of firearms.

At dawn I was awakened by a servant who brought tea and a small piece of Arab bread. After a short delay the horses were brought, my cook and I mounted, the guide followed afoot, and with loud cries of "Ya Allah" we turned our faces to the desert.

Sand! sand! sand!—everywhere sand! and as the sun rose higher the glare became blinding; but I drew my head-cloth well over my eyes and experienced little discomfort, except from my horse, which was blind on his port side and persisted in drifting to starboard. Troops of gazelles skimmed by, and ever and anon in the distance little oases of green grass would appear with small flocks of sheep feeding. The guide would invariably make a detour of these, fearing, he said, that we would be taken for soldiers going to collect the sheep tax, and that would mean a fusillade and a scamper. High mounds, all that remain of some ancient Chaldean city, were scattered about, each in turn serving as a landmark, and behind each in turn the guide promised that we should see the black tents of Sheikh Mithkal.

When we finally reached the place where his camp had been we found that Mithkal had moved two days to the south, so we pressed on, and at the next group of tents we paused for shelter. The sheikh came out to meet us, took my reins, and as I jumped from the saddle salaamed me warmly, and handing the horse to a servant led the way into the tent. The sun was still hot, but the cover of goats' hair gave sufficient shelter, and I stretched my weary limbs, thankful for so much of the journey over. The tribe soon gathered, the sheikh roasted, pounded and brewed the coffee at the door of the tent, and before long we were chatting in a friendly manner. I shall long remember with gratitude the gaunt Sheikh Nasif, rude and rough, but a gentleman at heart. Today as I sit in my room at Basrah, I can still imagine myself back in that camp, can see the travelling Persian merchant measuring out yards and yards of red and white Manchester cloth, the women busily pounding grain, and can still hear the rustle of the whispering "Sarahs" peeping at me through a hole in the flap that separated us from the harem.

At nightfall the horses were gathered and tethered in a circle within the camp, the fires were lighted and supper served—rice, a chicken, and a bowl of water. Careful questioning as to our whereabouts, aided by rough observations taken with a pocket compass, revealed the fact that we were then seventy-five miles due east from Jilat Sikr on the Shatt-el-Hai. The sheikh gave me a choice of sleeping in the tent or under the stars. For various reasons I chose to sleep in the open, and so my blanket was spread on the sand, and a coarse camels' hair pillow swarming with fleas given for my bed. I slept soundly that night despite the dew, which by morning had the effect of fine rain. At the first streak of dawn I was awakened by the bustle and stir of the women breaking camp. Tents were down and rolled up and all were waiting the sheikh's word to move.

And now the guide from Hataman became sullen and demanded more backsheesh. He did not know the rest of the way and he was afraid to go farther as there was a blood-feud on between his tribe and the marsh Arabs. But after the promise of a mejidie (a Turkish coin worth about eighty cents) he consented and we mounted and rode on to Hassan-el Hakkam, with whom canoes were most likely to be found. Three hours brought us to the edge of the swamp where sat poor Hassan, drowned out by the recent rains, smoking a disconsolate waterpipe. There the guide left us, after vainly trying to extort more backsheesh, to the tender mercies of the drowned-out sheikh.

It was now ten in the morning of Monday, and the needs of the inner man began to make themselves felt. Since the evening of Saturday we had had only one meal, and that had been short rations. Sheikh Hassan had anticipated my needs, however, and announced that after dinner I should be free to begin my swamp journey. With eager eyes I watched for the coming platter, and when it came my heart sank—a huge slab of rice-bread baked in dung ashes, hard as leather, and a decayed fish which gave notice of its presence from afar. I fell to for hospitality's sake and tried to be happy, but it was a failure. The mud-like slab would not go down, so to give the appearance of appreciation I slipped a huge chunk in my pocket, which I later shied at a mud-turtle. The fish still haunts me. A canoe was promised when the sun should have declined a little, and so we drearily waited in the goats' hair tent, gasping for air in that low-lying hollow, while the desert-flies stung like needles.

At four in the afternoon an old woman announced that her canoe was now at my service, so my box was shouldered, or rather "headed," and after a brief salaam we left Sheikh Hassan to complain of his hard luck, and started across the swamp. It was a really beautiful ride, no longer hot, the water fine and clear, the air fragrant with the odor of many marsh flowers, while gorgeous birds started up at our approach. For three hours we paddled steadily on, and then on asking whither I was being taken, I was abruptly told that on account of a recent feud, we should have to make a wide detour, and instead of going to Sheikh Soleima, were to be cast on Sheikh Mussellem. Just as the sun sank in the west Mussellem's camp hove in sight, the first of the real Ma'adan. Here and there a canoe lay idly swinging at its rope of twisted reeds, but for the rest, not a soul was in sight; suddenly we turned a corner and the canoe was cleverly beached in front of the sheikh's hut, lapped on four sides by water.

Mussellem himself stepped forward, a huge half naked savage, with hair to his shoulders. As he gave me his hand I said, "Dakhil" (I take refuge), and he quietly led the way into his hut. But no sooner had I become seated than the whole tribe gathered, looking like so many water rats: children entirely naked, women half, and men entirely, except for a breech-cloth. The hut was filled to suffocation; men, women, children crowding closer and closer and still coming. The first word the sheikh said was, "You are a deserting officer of the Turkish army." He no doubt had good reasons for his suspicions, as my cook resembled a soldier, and with my gaiters and khaki, and white head cloth, I looked considerably like some hard luck lieutenant.

At a word from the sheikh the hut was cleared and we were left alone. After five minutes he and five other men filed in, pointed at my box, and demanded to know its contents. I assured him that it contained medicine, that I was a travelling doctor seeking to please Allah by treating the sick free. So he brought forward a gray headed villain writhing in the agonies of colic, and said he would test my skill. Fortunately I had a bottle of morphine pills in my kit, and in five minutes the patient was calmly sleeping at my feet. My "skill" was indicated, and in a trice all the lame, blind and halt were summoned. The varieties of diseases treated by my twelve medicines would put an American practitioner to shame. Bicarbonate of soda, tonic and calomel, quinine and zinc sulphate, iodine, boracic acid and bromide covered the whole of the British pharmacopoeia.

At last the sheikh cried, "Enough!" ordered the crowd to disperse, and when they lingered, vigorously scattered them hither and thither with his huge fists and feet. Then for an hour we sat in front of the door of the hut on a mat, while two hundred of the tribe gathered in a close semicircle about me. In the background herds of water buffaloes snorted in the water. An old woman came up, gingerly touched my glasses, and asked if I had been born with them on. A huge savage, whom I had noticed come in with the sheikh when I was asked to open my box, put his finger on my heart, and slowly said:

"We had made up our minds to stab you there, but when we found you were a doctor we concluded to wait. Now you are safe, we trust you."

Cheering words, those! I quizzically asked whether my dakhil had not assured my safety, but he only answered, "We are Ma'adan."

Then the sheikh made a proposition. He would build me a hut, give me his niece, a girl of fourteen, to wife, and I must stay among them. The crowd murmured in approval. The bride would be brought the next morning and the ceremonies at once performed. I thanked the sheikh for his kindness, assured him that I would be proud to be his nephew, but that there was one great obstacle at present—my medicine was nearly gone. If he would treat me well and give me a canoe the next morning and help me on my way, I would proceed to Amarah, replenish my stock of drugs, and if God willed, return. (And I do want to return some day, if one of the mission doctors can go with me.) My excuse seemed reasonable, and Mussellem promised to let me go.

After a hearty supper of buffalo milk and rice, an entertainment was planned for my benefit. The bucks of the tribe gathered, and filled the hut to overflowing. In the center a bunch of reeds was kept burning for light, and at my side stood the performer. He sang of the deeds of his fathers, then of the disgrace of Sheikh Seihud, who had been routed two weeks before with a loss of two hundred men, in an invasion into these parts. Then the singer sang of my virtues and skill: I was tall and supple as a marsh reed, my eyes the eyes of a young buffalo, and so on. It was a strange sight, the rush fire fitfully lighting up the savage countenances and the antics of the singer, while the water pipe kept going the rounds.

That night I slept next to the plunder taken from Seihud a fortnight before. At dawn I asked permission to go; my box was hauled out, the canoe brought up, and when I wanted to embark a bear-like Ma'eidi quietly seated himself on my box and refused to let it go, saying it was to be held as a guarantee of my return. But the chief rudely kicked the intruder away and we were off, to be cast on the hospitality of Kheinuba two hours down. We passed up the small stream which here has separated itself from the marsh, past miles and miles of huts, and entered at last into the open lake beyond. The canoe was small, the wind had risen and the waves were high; the water came in by bucketfuls and I had already begun to calculate whether I could swim to the opposite shore now looming up in the haze. But a Ma'eidi is a skilled canoeist and he reached Kheinuba.

About half a mile from his hut we grounded the canoe to stop a leak, and then I bribed the big paddler in the stern to go on to the next camp, four hours away, where I had heard was a Nejdi Chief, Yusef, who had settled among the Ma'adan. A Nejdi is always an honorable host, less treacherous than the Ma'adan, and this particular one the most powerful chief in the whole district. We threw out the guide from Mussellem, gave him a tin tobacco box and told him to be quiet, and sped on to Yusef. Then the canoe turned into a rapid, turbulent river, on and on till Yusef's fort came into view—a huge mud structure bearing marks of the recent fracas. We landed opposite; I got out and walked into the mudhif (guest house) and sat in the guests' place. The whole concourse rose to salaam. I at once asked for a cigarette, and was safe, according to all rules of Arab etiquette. Although they speculated among themselves, and audibly, as to my identity and business, some questioned me

directly. A young Arab swore that he knew me as a distinguished officer of the Turkish army, and to this was attributed
my Arabic accent. Feigning weariness, I lay down and slept to
prevent further questioning. After a hearty dinner of rice and
mutton, a canoe was brought up, three armed men were sent
with us as guard, and we left Yusef's camp.

Up the river, hour after hour, we proceded past mud forts
recently shot to pieces, till near sunset the Turkish flag greeted
our eyes and we reached a military outpost. Never before was I
so glad to see the Star and Crescent, for it meant at any rate
safety—and bread. The Mudir welcomed us, brought tea,
brought supper, and then we climbed to the roof of his mud-
fort, for the air was close. Then he told me of the great battle of
the chiefs, how for ten days and nights the fusillade continued,
at night lighting up the sky like lightning, till at last Sheikh
Seihud retired, his power broken, his canoes shattered and the
flower of his tribe slaughtered. I could have hugged that kindly
Turk—no better host ever bade me welcome in an American
parlor. A thunder shower drove us from the roof, and that night
I slept regardless of fleas and mosquitoes, happy that so much
of the journey was over. The next morning I left in a large
canoe with towering bow, taking no guard, as the way was said
to be safe—twenty-five miles to Amarah. With us embarked an
Arab woman with four children and an infant. The sun was hot,
the dried skins in the canoe at my head fearfully odorous, the
flies tortured us, but Amarah was near and we minded nothing.
About ten miles below Amarah the Mujer-es-Saghir joins the
Tigris with a rush.

At its mouth we tied fast to the bank to get some milk from
a lowly cowherd, and the woman got out and walked along the
bank, carrying the infant. Suddenly six Arabs, armed with rifles,
appeared from the tall grass and came straight to the canoe.
They parleyed for a few minutes, then walked off in the
direction the woman had taken, who was now a hundred yards
ahead on the bank. Suddenly I heard a scream, and looking up
saw the six Arabs scampering off through the grass, carrying the
baby, waving their rifles and shouting a wild chant. The woman
came running up and said the child had been kidnapped for a
debt which her father owed to one of the Arabs. They had
trailed us from the fort and seized their opportunity when we
had tied to the bank. The Arabs were now far away in the grass,
and we could only faintly hear their yells in the distance, so we

decided to push on to Amarah and report the matter to the authorities. So on we crept again. Every few rods, Arabs would come to the bank and ask of Seihud's whereabouts. They had deserted him in his extremity, and were in hourly fear that he would return to slaughter them.

At four in the afternoon we reached Amarah. The missionary and not a government expedition had drawn a fine red line across the blank space on the map.

The next chapter of these desert adventures is comprised of the trips made with Sir William Willcocks. He had a staff of English engineers under him and eventually made a most comprehensive report to the Turkish Government. He proposed an extensive series of large works, and these recommendations, with the set of drawings and designs appended to it, remain up to the present time the basic source of reference on irrigation development in Iraq.

Sir William was a devout Christian, and took as his starting point the well-known account in Genesis 2:7-15 of the four rivers which went out of Eden. One was the Hiddekel, the Tigris of today—now an independent stream, because the channel became silted up. A second was the Euphrates. The third, the Gihon, is now the Hindiyeh, a broad deep stream which encircles the land of Cush (the Casii).

"But where," demanded the great engineer, "is the Pishon?"

He said that the first three rivers would not have been sufficient to carry off the discharge of the volume of water coming down the main parent river, and vowed that he would authenticate the Bible account of the fourth river. He had a good idea of where it might be.

Together Sir William and John rode out into the stark uninhabited desert, and suddenly the expert's keen eye detected the contour and deposits for which he was looking.

"There it is!" he cried—and the ancient channel of the Pishon of Old Testament fame was identified by the modern man of science.

In the course of their journeys, Willcocks had occasion to consult government officials at every town and village and isolated post, to extract all possible information. He knew Arabic but was more familiar with Egyptian colloquial than that of Mesopotamia, and depended on John to be his interpreter. Often a zealous official would tell Sir William what he thought the strange Englishman wanted to know, rather than bare facts.

"Tell him he darkens counsel with words!" he shouted irascibly on one such occasion.

"The Beg says," translated John, "that you don't quite understand what he wishes to know."

"Look here, Van Ess, you aren't telling him what I said," accused the "Beg" impatiently.

"Sir William," replied John deferentially, "I shall probably come back here some day on my own, without the prestige and authority of you and your experts, and I can't afford to antagonize these fellows."

The two agreed that the Tree of Life was undoubtedly the date tree; and the Tree of the Knowledge of Good and Evil was the vine.

John thought that the flaming sword with which the angel drove Adam out of Paradise was salt. This would have ruined the Garden because man neglected to flush the soil after he became drunk on the wine which he so disastrously made from the fruit of the vine.

Sir William's theory was that the flaming sword was bitumen and naphtha springs, accidently set alight. This might also have been the "pillar of fire by night," and perhaps the pillar of cloud by day was a whirling "dust devil."

The first of Willcocks' recommendations to the Turkish Government was to build the Hindiyeh Barrage. This was completed before 1914. Over the years since then, his long range planning for flood control and irrigation has continuously been carried out in Iraq.

Travelling with this distinguished and companionable Englishman was a very rich experience for young John Van Ess.

That it was advantageous also to Sir William was expressed in his own words in his *Sixty Years in the East*.

Seeing the country on the lower Euphrates and the lower Tigris in the Basrah Vilayet so very hostile to the Turks, I was nervous about sending engineers there and mentioned the fact to Mr. Van Ess, the American missionary. He said he would get a pass from the Muntefik Arabs which would ensure the safety of the survey parties over the whole vilayet, and he was as good as his word. We surveyed the country during two seasons, and we were never molested. The Wali was jealous of our moving freely where no Turks were allowed to go, and eventually insisted on our leaving the country before the survey was finished, on the plea that our lives were in danger. As a matter of fact he thought we were intriguing, and he insisted on our leaving the plans and levels unfinished, probably owing to orders from Constantinople.

On his own John Van Ess made a tour of the Pirate Coastal region—now called the Trucial Coast, as piracy had long been suppressed by the British patrol. Here John stayed with a pearl merchant, and was fascinated by the lore of that romantic traffic.

In 1906 he went further afield in the summer, travelling by British India ship to Bombay and thence third class by Messagerie Maritime to Beirut. He had a thoroughly enjoyable sojourn in Lebanon, making his headquarters in Beirut. Here he settled in a little pension on a road above the sea front and was soon quite at home. One morning he went into the dining room and took his usual seat, where his breakfast was promptly brought by a waiter who greeted him in Arabic.

Some Dutch monks who were sitting at a nearby table commented in their own language,

"You can tell that is an American because he gets what he wants right away."

What was their astonishment when John turned and said to them in Dutch, "So could you, if you knew how to ask for it."

From Lebanon he proceeded to Constantinople (now called Istanbul) with the intention of studying Turkish. He had achieved a working knowledge of it from his many friends among the Turkish officials in the Basrah and Baghdad provinces and wanted to "put a polish on it," as he expressed it. He found congenial lodging at Robert College on the glorious hills overlooking the Bosphorus and spent pleasant and profitable weeks there. He used to ride the ferryboats on the river every day, sitting as close as possible to the section reserved for women, because he said the most beautiful Turkish in the world was that spoken by the Khanums—the ladies of the harems—and he strained his ears to hear the melodious sounds of their conversation and catch their accent.

On his return journey to Basrah he travelled from Meskene, near Aleppo, six hundred miles down the Euphrates to Felluja by raft. This was a substantial structure about twenty-five feet

square, built upon inflated goat skins, with a sweep on each side
to keep it in midstream, and an extra long one added to the
stern for a rudder when they reached the rapids. A cargo of
soap was taken on for ballast, passengers were accepted on
condition that they would help man the sweeps, and at Felluja
the soap was delivered and the raft sold at a profit.

It was during this term that John's touring often took him to
the vicinity of Kerbala and Nejf, two of the cities most ven-
erated by Shiah Muslims. Here he had opportunity to meet the
Mujtahids—the equivalent of the College of Cardinals in Shiah
Islam. Their spiritual and temporal power was tremendous and
they were highly educated within the circumscribed scope of
their narrow and inflexible theology. They were expertly
trained in debate and disputation, and they found young Van
Ess a worthy opponent in theological discussion. He greatly
enjoyed pitting his wits against their keen minds and found the
intellectual exercise of what is technically called "The Muslim
Controversy" stimulating and exhilarating. He learned during
these years, however, that this fascinating mental experience
had little value from a missionary point of view and that there
were more affirmative and effective ways of presenting the
Christian way of life.

His roving assignment during these years when John was on
his own gave him wide experience of the Arabs in both towns
and tribes. In the station he learned to know officials of the
Turkish Government and to understand their ways. Outside
Mesopotamia he made many contacts in the mission area bor-
dering the Persian Gulf. One of his last expeditions before he
went on furlough was to visit Kuwait with a view of gaining a
foothold there for the Mission.

When he got back to America he shaved off his beard, got a
whole outfit of new clothes and proceeded to enjoy his own
country to the full. On one of his first journeys by train he
presented his clergy ticket—at that time available for half fare—
and was promptly challenged by the conductor. This official
gave a searching look at the young man in a jaunty flannel suit,
with his Panama hat at a rakish angle, and said grimly,

"What are you trying to do, brother, bum a ride? You look
more like a race track sport than a minister."

John protested his honesty and produced his clergy certifi-
cate, with his signature.

"Anyone can learn to fake a signature to save the fare from New York to Chicago," persisted the still suspicious conductor.

"All right," replied John indignantly, and pulled a small Testament from his pocket. "You choose a text and I'll preach you a sermon. I'll show you whether I'm a clergyman or not!"

VI

Under the Star and Crescent

I first saw Basrah under a full moon on the last night of 1911. We went up the Shatt-el-Arab river by launch from Mohammerah (now Khoramshar) on the Persian side, a trip of about eighteen miles. Majestic date palms lined both sides of the river, a glorious sight in the moonlight, and there was an occasional Arab village to be seen as we swept along and, now and then, the large country house of some wealthy landowner.

Presently we came to Ashar Creek, at right angles to the river, with the Turkish Custom House at the corner. This was the principal waterway of the city and connected the port section of town, Ashar, with old Basrah City, a mile or more west of the river. As we turned into the creek I could see the dome and minaret of a large mosque, pale and beautiful against the moonlit sky. The roofs of the bazaars were visible behind the mosque, and as we went on up the creek we passed the closely built Arab city along the water front. The houses looked like fairy palaces in the moonlight, the bridges under which we went on our way to the mission house were bathed in enchantment, the date palms were stately and tranquil. Though I knew it afterwards in prosaic daylight and devoid of all glamor, I have never forgotten the loveliness of my first impression of the city which was to be my home for nearly half a century.

John and I had been married in Chicago the previous June. I had gone home from Bahrain because of the death of my father. At the early age of forty-nine he had succumbed to pernicious anemia. My only consolation was that John had been with my family during these sad weeks and had been an inestimable comfort to them. He had learned to know my wonderful father well and they had fortified each other's faith.

We sailed to England in November, crossed to Holland for a brief visit to see the homeland of John's forebears, and then we went by train across Europe to Constantinople. This was my first sight of the magical city on the Bosphorus, then the capital of the great Ottoman Empire. It was just as romantic and appealing as I had imagined it, and I was thrilled to visit Robert

College, remembering my childhood encounter with its founder, Cyrus Hamlin.

Another ship carried us across the Aegean to Egypt, where we went by train from Alexandria to Cairo. I saw the sights, well known to John from previous visits—the Pyramids and Sphinx, the Citadel and mosques, and the fascinating bazaars—and we enjoyed the companionship of our missionary friends. From Suez we travelled on a cargo ship down the Red Sea, around the Arabian peninsula, and up the Persian Gulf to the mouth of the great Shatt-el-Arab.

This noble "River of the Arabs" is formed by the junction of the Tigris and Euphrates rivers a hundred miles up from the sea. It is navigable by ocean-going ships as far up as Basrah, the port of Iraq. From Basrah to Baghdad, the only connection in those early days was by river ships, flatbottomed side-wheeler steamers with a draft of five feet.

The whole countryside was intersected with creeks, and smaller canals led off them, through which the tide rose and fell twice in twenty-four hours. Though the river is tidal, the water is fresh and the date gardens flourish in this bountiful provision of nature. Little villages are strung along the creeks and canals, like beads on a chain. There were few roads then and all local transportation was by bellum—comfortable boats, something between a canoe and a gondola, manned by two stalwart boatmen called bellumjes (a Turkish adaptation). They rowed or poled the boat according to the tide.

Up one of these creeks we went on that moonlight night, till we reached the mission house where our colleagues awaited us, and a new chapter in our joint life was to begin.

The political setting for our lives, in those last years of the great Ottoman Empire, was a dramatic one, a period of transition between an old world about to pass away and a new and totally different one about to be born.

When John first went to Basrah in 1902 the country which is now called Iraq was under the autocratic rule of Sultan Abdul Hamid. "The Land Between the Rivers" was the richest he possessed and he guarded it jealously, keeping a large army there, many of them Albanian and Kurdish troops on whose loyalty he could depend. Arab subjects of the Empire were also conscripted for military service, many being obliged to serve for seven years. Arab tribes were continually revolting against the hated Ottoman rule.

A bellum on the Basrah Creek

For hundreds of years the Arabs had been included in the
Turkish Empire and had accepted it unquestioningly as the
guardian of Islam. When the great Abbasid dynasty in Iraq came
to an end in 1258, and the Mongolian conqueror Hulaku,
grandson of Genghis Khan, destroyed Baghdad, Arab history
reached one of its lowest points. For three centuries Iraq was
governed by the Mongol emperors of Iran and their successors:
Timur the Lame, Turkoman rulers, and the Safawi Persians.
Then Sulaiman the Magnificent captured Baghdad and Mosul in
1535 and added them to the mighty Ottoman Empire which
already included Syria, Egypt and Arabia.

Henceforth the Arabs, as Muslims, were proud of the power
and prestige of the Ottoman Empire and identified themselves
with it. It was theirs as much as it was the Turks'. How often I
heard old ladies exclaim during my early years in Basrah,

"Allah yansir el Din wa e' Doulat!" (May God make victori-
ous the Religion and the State!)

They were one and inseparable.

The Sultan of Turkey was also the Caliph of all Islam, the
Successor of the Prophet, the Pontiff of Muslims, the Shadow

of God. He was the Protector of the two Holy Cities of Mecca and Medina in Arabia, the places of pilgrimage for all Muslims throughout the world.

The status quo had been taken for granted for centuries, and it was only in the latter years of the reign of the despot Abdul Hamid, when corruption and misgovernment had become the rule, that dissatisfaction began to be felt.

John wrote of conditions in 1902:

There was no security. Robberies were common and a person did not venture far from the city after sunset . . . .The schools were few and very poorly equipped. In them no Arabic was taught at all. Turkish was the language of instruction. Many teachers, and always the director of education of the province, knew no Arabic. Freedom was non-existent. No books, magazines or newspapers were allowed except those that had no value. Foreigners were under the jurisdiction of their own consuls. In the British Consulate was a post office by means of which magazines and newspapers came to me from Egypt and other countries. On Fridays I used to go in a bellum across the Shatt-el-Arab river and there I would meet ten or twelve sons of some of the good families of Basrah. They would sit and read for two hours from the books and magazines which I had brought. At the end of that time I would hide the books under my coat and we would each go to his home.

There were no railroads in the country at all. The nearest railway was that between Damascus and Beirut. On the river Tigris were steamers which connected Baghdad with Basrah. In the spring when the current was strong it might take a week or more to reach Baghdad. When the water was low in the autumn it might take two weeks or more.

There were no hospitals and very few doctors. Every four years cholera or plague took thousands of lives. The present treatment for the prevention of these diseases was then unknown. The different religious sects would gather in the desert at the Zobeir Gate and implore Allah to protect them from death. There was, of course, no electricity nor any motor cars. The gramophone was regarded as a miracle and in the minds of many it was magic.

Quarantine rules were erratic. They could be very strict, especially if there was plague or cholera in India, or they could be relaxed if the right official had his "palm greased." At John's first mission meeting in Basrah there was a cholera scare and everyone had to stay in quarantine several days, so they held their meeting "Under the Yellow Flag" as he gleefully entitled his report.

Sir William Willcocks graphically describes one crisis:

In September and October cholera broke out everywhere, and the Turks had a splendid opportunity for harassing everybody. Iraq put the whole world into quarantine, and every town and village put every other town or village likewise into quarantine . . . . One of my engineers, coming from England, did five days quarantine at Basrah, five to get into Baghdad, and five more to get out of it; and if he had come a fortnight later he would have had another five days at the Hindia Barrage, as the right bank of the Barrage put the left in quarantine. The Wali reduced the pay of all the doctors by one half, as he said they had splendid opportunities for adding to their income.

Living under such conditions was frustrating and soul-wearying, but in after years John was glad that he had known the old Turkish regime at first hand, before it passed into history. He was fond of the Turks as individuals and made some good friends, and he was shrewd at observing and assessing the way they operated as officials.

John knew the Turkish pashas well who came to Basrah as governors of the Province. Most of them were a disillusioned, cynical lot, hating the exile from Istanbul and concerned chiefly in getting back, with interest, the money they had spent to secure the post.

Hassan Bey remarked one day to my husband,

"I have been here thirteen months, and how much do you think I have accumulated? Eighteen thousand liras!"

A lira was a Turkish gold pound, which fluctuated in value around five dollars.

"You are surprised?" continued the pasha,

By heaven, I paid five thousand liras to get this job, and I may be deposed tomorrow and sent back to Istanbul. There I shall have to pay another five or six thousand liras to get another post. Do not misjudge us. We do not claim to govern the country. We aim to line our pockets.

On the whole Hassan Bey and his like treated Europeans agreeably enough, so long as complaints and petitions were not made through official channels. In fact, inability to get along with foreigners was always sure to set a black mark against any Turk aspiring to a governorship, and consequently an official letter or a personal visit generally cleared the way for any European to accomplish ends not too blatantly illegal.

Pass from the civil to the military pasha and you meet again with the identical breed, the difference one of degree only, but as great as the difference between the frock coat which the former affected, and the spurred boots and tight jacket of the latter. With this uniform and fiercely curled mustachios, every official added to his title what is called "swank."

Then there were the "date pashas." Old Hajji Ibrahim was an Arab and the owner of large date estates. He was a "Pasha el Tamr," a date pasha, as the local wags called him and his kind. He paid the recognized price of two hundred and fifty pounds for his title, which included his uniform, made specially for him in Stamboul.

My husband described him with gusto, as he appeared when paying an official call on the governor:

Being an Arab and accustomed to free flowing garments, capacious cotton breeches and sandals, his whole posture and gait spelled acute and conscious misery as he would come stumping in with tight trousers, tighter patent leather shoes, snug long-tailed coat with high collar, white cotton gloves and fez that sank over his ears, while his dragging sword threatened to trip him at every step and his decoration dangled grandly. Slowly and carefully he would come into the salon, make his bow and salute, and proceed to sit down very circumspectly, acutely aware of the possibility of disaster to the seat of his trousers.

The Serai, where the governor received his visitors, was an establishment that beggars description. It was the Government House, the headquarters for the vilayet or province of Basrah. All departments were located here, with the wali, or governor, at the head. Treasury, justice, police, education, pious foundations, deeds, Crown lands—all had their offices in one dilapidated building.

The Serai was invariably a ramshackle affair. The corridors were dark and indescribably dirty, the rooms shabby and squalid. Here came the great and the near-great: officials, gentry, and the general public, to pay their respects to the governor on official holidays, such as the *Eed el Jaloos* or Feast of the Accession.

The customs was another department which tried the soul, especially in the matter of clearing books. It is amusing in retrospect but it was exasperating and maddening at the time. A missionary imported some English primers for use in his school. These, as all books, were subject to examination by the censor. Imagine the horror of the missionary when he saw on the first page of the primer the picture of a dog, and under it in large accusing letters, "THIS IS MY DOG. HIS NAME IS TURK." The censor had, years before, for six months run a restaurant on Liberty Street in New York City and knew a smattering of English. The book was at once taken to the pasha who sat within.

"A dog named Turk!" shrieked he. "Allah! What blasphemy!"

"But, Excellency," said the missionary soothingly, "listen and I shall explain. In America a dog is much thought of. Even the women sometimes carry him in their arms. He is a precious animal and so we give him a precious name. The Censor Effendi has been in America. He knows it. What, Censor Effendi, is it not so?"

The censor effendi swelled perceptibly. He rose grandly to the occasion.

"Excellency, the effendi speaks the truth. It is even so. I have seen it with these two eyes." Only then did the pasha relax.

"Wallah, even I do not know everything!" said he. "Pardon, effendi; I was only consumed by patriotism. Take your books. I thank you for the compliment you pay us in them."

Then they had sherbet and coffee and parted the best of friends.

We had it on the authority of a former consul general at Beirut that some chemistry text books were seized and confiscated because the formula H_2O was interpreted to hint darkly that Hamid the Second was a zero quantity.

Photographic plates were as a rule opened and examined *en plein jour* lest the boxes contain seditious literature.

Turkish law courts recognized no corporations and consequently all property had to be held in the name of an individual. I collided with this law when trying to register some property in the name of the New York corporation which was the real owner, and so I consulted the leading lawyer in the city.

"Pay me twenty liras," said he, "and I will get it registered in the name of any company of men, jinns, or devils, and cursed be the forbears and progeny of any man who dares to say me nay."

I did not pay the price, but I am confident that the transaction would have been less questioned than many a legitimate item in the law book, thanks to the pasha who was the patron of this particular lawyer. In justice to the Turks we must admit that the probate courts were administered on the whole justly and promptly. The Koran is very explicit on the subject of the right of orphans, and I think the officials honestly tried to conform to its injunctions.

The Department of Education specialized not so much in the liberal arts as it expected the art of liberality in return for service and expedition. In the parlance of the land it was called the Circle of the Sciences. To one who had to sit hours, days, weeks, awaiting the pleasure of the director, the Circle was an eternity. The officials who presided over this bureau might all have been cut out by a cookie cutter, they were so much alike. They knew only Turkish, a distinct annoyance in a land where Arabic was the prevailing tongue.

The teachers were on the whole inefficient, coarse and crude, shunning hard work and suspicious of everyone.

The Turkish schools suffered of course from such direction. Their curriculum was comprehensive enough and some of the teachers had fair mental equipment. Sometimes graduates were turned out who were creditable enough. But the moral surroundings were so shocking that it is no wonder Turkey was morally bankrupt. For a maund of dates (about eight pounds) any pupil could buy a promotion. Upon the least pretext the slow or recalcitrant pupil was pulled up short with a flow of language from the teacher.

"Dog, son of sixteen dogs!" and so on till it becomes unprintable.

Dirk Dykstra of the mission one day wandered into a school in a small town up the Tigris River. On the wall hung a map of the Western Hemisphere. The class was being taught something about the New World. The teacher, knowing his visitor was an American, asked him to tell something of his homeland. So Dirk pointed to the Isthmus of Panama and told of the canal and the project of uniting two oceans. When he was through the teacher stepped forward with the following cogent moral:

"This teaches us how privileged we are to live in a land where Allah is known and feared. Over there they purpose to cross Allah's path by making water to flow where He made land."

But Dirk's comeback took the wind out of the mullah's sails.

"I see," said he, "you have made a bridge across the Tigris river here. If Allah had wanted you to walk to the other side why did He separate you from it by a river?"

A teacher in a government school was looking through a magazine which displayed the picture of a typewriter. When I explained to him the functions of a typewriter and the advantage of its use he looked mystified. Finally a great light seemed to dawn.

"Ah, yes," he remarked. "That is a fine invention. I see it now. It is for such as cannot read or write."

The Imperial Ottoman Navy is a subject in itself. The Sultan was being entertained by the antics of a sword swallower.

"Wonderful, wonderful!" he exlaimed. "I have never seen anything more wonderful."

"If it please your majesty," said a courtier, "I have seen the Ministry of Marine swallow a whole battleship."

In brief, that is where most of the projected navy went.

In past days the visitor to Constantinople saw anchored in the Golden Horn three formidable looking battleships but it was well known that all the "innards" had long since been removed. Old Abdul Hamid in his Yildiz Palace on the Bosphorus cherished a mortal fear of his own navy, but kept up this empty show to impress populace and tourist.

In Basrah river lay the "Klid Bahr," Lock of the Sea. She was a hoary relic and had been anchored from time out of mind. A rebellion broke out in Qatar,* a then desolate fever-ridden peninsula in the Persian Gulf, and the "Klid Bahr" was ordered thither. Consternation reigned at the office of the commodore. The chief engineer, who had grown gray in the service, came in with a dirty slip of paper listing among the desiderata for the

---

* In the 1970's sons of Qatar attend the alma mater of John Van Ess, Hope College, in considerable numbers and considerable affluence.

voyage three hundred barrels of cement to case the boilers. After days of feverish haste, H.M.S. "Klid" tried to start. But the anchor, so long embedded in the soft mud of the river, had sunk to join the anchors of Sindbad who sailed these waters centuries before. So the cable was cut, a new anchor fastened on, and with many cries of "Ya Allah!" they started. With sails and a fair wind and full steam ahead they reached Qatar on the sixth day. I was assured of this from Jabr Agha, the old quarter-master who went along. The "Klid" now reposes on the bottom of the river where she was sunk by the Turks in October, 1914, to close the channel against the British. The sister ship of the "Klid" was ordered to Constantinople. After many vicissitudes she reached the Dardanelles and the crew, every man jack of them, were decorated for the feat of getting her there. They deserved it.

The Imperial Navy in those waters also boasted a river patrol boat, called the "Alus." I was on the "Alus" once for a week as the guest of Lieutenant Nuri Effendi. Poor fellow, he was also one of those who had been ambitious. Petition after petition he sent in to the Admiralty begging for service anywhere, just so he would not rust out. The engines of the boat were dated 1867. When the "Alus" got up steam one fine day to change her anchorage, I went ashore and stayed overnight, till she stopped breathing again.

A new era began in 1908 when the Young Turk Party achieved a bloodless revolution under the Committee of Union and Progress. They forced the Sultan to restore the Midhat Constitution of 1876, suppressed by him for thirty-two years. A Parliament was summoned and the first meeting took place at the end of the year in the presence of Sultan Abdul Hamid and the Ottoman princes. At first this happy event was taken at its face value and "Abdul the Damned" became "Abdul the Blessed."

But the Sultan of the dying Empire (sometimes called in international circles "The Sick Man of Europe") was privately determined to get rid of the Young Turks, Constitution, and new Parliament, and in the spring of 1909 there was an attempt at a counter-revolution in Istanbul. The army in Macedonia marched on the capital and laid siege to Yildiz Palace, the Sultan's residence; Parliament and Senate met and voted the deposition and exile of Abdul Hamid, and put his brother

Mohammed Rashad in his place as Sultan Mohammed V. This royal figurehead held the title until 1918. He was succeeded by Vahid-el-Din as Mohammed VI and in 1923 Turkey became a Republic.

Arab national consciousness had been growing throughout the years and societies had been established in different parts of the Ottoman Empire, especially in Lebanon and Syria, to promote recognition and independence for the Arabs. In Constantinople itself a secret group called Al Ahd (The Covenant) was formed by army officers who were Arabs (Iraqis being most prominent), pledged to work for Arab independence. When the despot was removed and the Young Turks came into power the shackles of the past seemed to be broken. An effort was made to secure political autonomy for Arab districts, and Arab representation in the Imperial Government at Istanbul on a basis of full equality with Ottoman Turks.

An Arab-Syrian Congress at Paris in 1913 urged among other resolutions that the Arabic language be recognized in the Ottoman Parliament and considered an official language in Syrian and Arab countries. It also recommended that military service should be regional in Syrian and Arab vilayets except in extreme necessity.

The cause of Arab nationalism was advanced in Basrah Vilayet and throughout Turkish Arabia (now Iraq) chiefly through the energy and determination of one man. Sayyid Talib Pasha was the son of Sayyid Rejib, the Naqib of Basrah. The Naqib is the head of all Sayyids (direct descendants of the Prophet) and the keeper of their records in his vicinity. Sayyid Talib was the representative for Basrah vilayet in the Turkish Parliament at Constantinople and made both friends and enemies in the Committee of Union and Progress. He had also been Mutcsserrif of Al Hasa on the Arabian mainland, then part of the Ottoman Empire. After the Revoluation of 1908 from which he and other Arabs all over the Empire had expected such great things, he turned against the C.U.P. and joined forces with the Moderate Liberal Party and later with the Hurriyah wa Itilaf.

In 1911 he and a group of Arab deputies appealed to Sherif Hussein of Mecca to "Shake the yoke which weighed on the Arabs and to deliver them from tyranny and slavery."

Early in 1913 a meeting at his house was attended by all the leading Arabs of Basrah who drew up a petition later signed by three hundred prominent citizens. This asked permission to summon a Provincial Council which should prepare a scheme of reforms needed in the vilayet and what amounted to local autonomy.

Soon after, in March 1913, an Arab Conference was held in Mohammerah (now Khoramshahr). This was attended by the Sheikh of Mohammerah, Khazel (an Arab, although technically under Persian suzerainty), the Sheikh of Kuwait (the great Mobarek), Sayyid Talib, and a leading Turkish official. Their goal was to advance Iraq to self-government and eventually to independence. They sent messengers to Kerbala and Nejf to stir up the people there. These great Shiah centers felt no loyalty to the Sunni Turks and had always resented their leadership in the Muslim world. Information about these activities was sent to Arab nationalists in Baghdad, Constantinople, Syria, Egypt, and Arabia, with whom Sayyid Talib was in correspondence.

In the meantime the "Turkifying" efforts of the Young Turk Party were in full force, and their attempt was to carry out a Pan-Turanian policy throughout the Empire and suppress all Arab aspirations.

In June, 1913, a gendarme commander named Ferid Beg was sent to Basrah presumably to kill Sayyid Talib and several other Arab leaders. He was assassinated upon his arrival, undoubtedly by followers of the pasha. John and I were sitting on our roof and some of the spent bullets whizzed past our heads. When we were told later what had happened our informant said grimly,
    "Sayyid Talib got him first!"

Sayyid Talib Pasha was a vigorous and colorful personality and a real leader of men. He was a warm personal friend of my husband's and mine and did us many good turns over the years. I knew his four wives well—one Arab one, the daughter of Naqib of Kuwait, a beautiful and queenly lady; and three charming Circassians who all lived in one huge establishment in Basrah City in those early days. I knew all the children and have always kept up my friendship with the Pasha's numerous descendants. He was a friend and champion of the poor and underprivileged and a ruthless exploiter of the rich. He was always suspected of placing his personal ambition above his patriotism, and justly or unjustly this was to affect his whole future career.

In spite of all these political cross currents, or perhaps because of them, there was a much freer and more relaxed atmosphere in Basrah when I went there in 1911 than when John first knew it in 1902.

It was a Muslim country and one was always fully conscious of that fact, but the Christian and Jewish minorities lived amicably and unmolested—as the Jews had done since Babylonian times. The Christians were members of the various branches of the historic Oriental churches which survived the great invasion of Islam. The upper classes were chiefly Sunni Muslims, like the Turks, but there was a large Shiah population and the great Shiah shrines at Kerbela and Nejf were at the height of their prestige and power. Pilgrims from Persia, an almost wholly Shiah country, visited them, and likewise Indian Muslims. Conspicuous on the creek front near the river in Basrah was a large khan for Indian pilgrims, Shiahs on their way to Kerbela and Nejf. They were shepherded by their custodians and interpreters from the British India ships to await embarkation for up country on the river paddle steamers and their bewildered alien figures were a familiar sight whenever a ship was in.

The economy of Iraq was agricultural, as it had been for many centuries, and we in Basrah were in the midst of the world's greatest date plantation. The entire country had suffered grievously when the ancient irrigation systems were destroyed in the Mongol invasions in the thirteenth century, and the appointment of Sir William Willcocks by the Turkish government to draw up and carry out a scheme of modern scientific irrigation gave a bright hope for the future.

Another project which would have eventually helped to transform the country was the proposed Berlin-Baghdad railway. This would have revived ancient trade routes and made Iraq once more a "Crossroads of the world"! Political and financial consideration slowed down the execution of the plan until after World War I but the idea was prominent in people's minds during the last years of Turkish rule.

The social structure of Islam dominated the country. Townsmen and tribesmen were sharply divided in their loyalties and interests. The wealth of the few and the abject poverty of the many were accepted with the fatalism of Islam. So was disease, malnutrition, crime, and the inferior position of women. This was the world into which I entered on the last day of the old year, 1911.

The colleagues who welcomed us in Basrah were old friends. They were the Rev. and Mrs. James Cantine, who had been like parents to me on the long voyage from America, when Christine Iverson and I had been fortunate enough to travel under their wing, and Arthur Bennett and Christine (now Mrs. Bennett), both doctors and in charge of the joint men's and women's hospitals.

There were no other hospitals in Basrah then, and few doctors. A Turkish Army doctor, Greek by origin, was said to eliminate any patient whose ill-wishers made it worth his while, no questions asked. He was an implacable enemy of our mission hospital and of our work in general. Yet curiously enough when he died in 1917 his last request was that Mr. Van Ess conduct his funeral and bury him. With a good deal of difficulty John arranged for him to be buried in the courtyard of the Armenian Church.

Our mission hospital had very little trouble in establishing itself. Our doctors had Turkish diplomas obtained in Constantinople after a nominal examination. The up-to-date hospital and clinic filled a great need and was eagerly patronized by rich and poor alike. The medical work was flourishing and was a great asset for the prestige of the whole mission.

The Cantines lived in a charming old Arab house across the creek from the hospital compound. James Cantine was in charge of our colporteurs and Bible shop and of the evangelistic program for the whole region and conducted Sunday services in Arabic and English. Mrs. Cantine had a wide acquaintance with Arab women of all classes and did a great deal of welfare work in a quiet and unostentatious way. Their home was an "open house" for all comers, Arab and foreign. No senior colleagues could have been more helpful to their juniors and we were a most happy and congenial group.

Very soon John and I were established in our own home, a delightful Arab house similar to the Cantines', farther up the creek. These were of yellow brick, built around a courtyard with spacious inside verandahs on the second floor where our living rooms were. Downstairs were our kitchens, storerooms, and servants' quarters. On the flat roofs we slept in summer, and used the corner of the roof where we could overlook the road as an after-sundown sitting room.

Our household staffs were a grand assortment. We, like most foreigners, had Goanese cooks. They came from a tiny Portuguese colony on the west coast of South India, and had a trip back to their homes and families once in two years. John and I had an Afghan house servant, a legacy from his bachelor days. The Cantines had a Negro houseboy and the Bennetts an Arab—

both of whom remained in mission service as long as they lived. Most of our British friends had Indian butlers and houseboys. Our boatmen were all tribal Arabs, who lived in a settlement across the river. They brought our fresh water every morning from the middle of the river (we hoped, at high tide!) and the whole bellum was filled with drums and oil tins to provide us with our daily supply. They were also our messengers and errand men as there were no telephones; and since there were very few roads we went everywhere by bellum.

The weekly "fast boat" of the British India Steamship Company which connected with the P. and O. in Bombay brought us our mail; and the "slow boat" which meandered up the Gulf from India, stopping at every port on both the Arabian and Persian side, was our means of communicating with our colleagues down the Gulf. Our news came to us by favor of Reuters, which circulated all copies of their news telegrams received at the Indo-European telegraph station at Fao, at the mouth of the Shatt-el-Arab.

The foreign community consisted of British, German, Russian and Belgian consuls with their families and staffs; and representatives of shipping firms (the majority of them British), the chief one being Gray and Mackenzie, who represented the British India S. S. Company. Dates and grain were the chief exports of the country. One spectacular year, when there had been an epidemic among the sheep up country, an enterprising Dutchman came and bought up all the sheep intestines, which make particularly good sausage casings.

The French consular agent was Count Asfar, leading member of a great Arab Christian clan. They were devout and generous Catholics (his title was a Papal one) and most of them were educated in France and England. They had large land holdings and business interests throughout the country. Count Asfar used frequently to be my partner at badminton at the pleasant "At Homes" held weekly during the summer months by the various consulates and firms. I still recall vividly his erect figure in white tennis flannels and invariable red cummerbund as he moved nimbly about the court.

We had a branch of the Imperial Ottoman Bank in Basrah, with a French manager; and there was a little Greek shop where we used to buy black olives and sardines and mysterious preserves. We lived as much as possible off the local bazaar and made good use of such things as dates and the delicious date syrup called "dibbis," pomegranate juice and the many excellent native cereals, but we sent twice a year for a large grocery order from London of staples not then obtainable in Basrah.

Life was comfortable and pleasant and the pace was moderate. We each had our own work to do which was absorbing and interesting and fully occupied our time and energy. But outside pressures had not yet begun to build up. We set our own schedule and operated happily within it.

As soon as we were settled the next step was to open schools for both boys and girls. John had been working for years for the government permits which were now in hand. He began the boys' school in the spring of 1912. I had to finish my language work, which had been interrupted by my return to America, so that I was six months behind the students of my year. Wearily I toiled on, preparing for my final examinations in June. Sometimes I asked John's help on a difficult point of grammar. On one of these occasions he said:

"Oh, don't bother with that, it would never be asked in an examination."

Indignantly I replied:

"But they *did* ask it on Christine's and the Calverleys' examination paper!"

"Well, they had no business to!" was his unfeeling answer. "I make it a point never to set a question that I would have to look up myself. I bet those fellows consulted the grammar for that one. It was absurd to ask it."

Cold comfort for me, who for years was to say "They make us do thus-and-so" when describing our mission Arabic requirements, whereas John would always say "We have our candidates do such-and-such work."

I did finish eventually and enjoyed a lighthearted and carefree summer, full of anticipation and plans for opening the girls' school in the autumn.

VII

Schools of High Hope

The School of High Hope was the official name of the Basrah boys' school—*Medrissa el Reja' el Ali*, and the girls' school was The School of Hope for Girls—*Medrissa el Rija' l'il Benat*.

John Van Ess had been working on the preliminaries for obtaining the permits long before I knew him, the mission having assigned him the task because he had acquired a certain adroitness in dealing with the "Wily Turk," who could be such a good friend personally but so maddening as an official.

In 1912, when he at last was able to open the boys' school, John wrote:

"The story of how the Imperial 'Firman' was at last obtained would take pages to relate. At length I emerged from the labyrinth of negotiation with the precious document embellished with the Sultan's signature in gold ink."

There had been much merriment in the mission when they first heard that I had been appointed, and that a young woman named "Firman" was coming out for school work. The coincidence was considered a good omen.

In 1913 I wrote a report setting forth the story of this long drawn-out saga, which has the value of contemporary account:

The well known rule for rabbit pie, which begins with the words "First catch your rabbit," may well be applied to the rule for making a school in the Turkish Empire. "First get your permission." There is much unwritten history concerning all the mission enterprises which have been attempted within the jurisdiction of the Sublime Ottoman Government, and perhaps the founders of schools, more than anyone else, could tell many tales: of petitions pigeon-holed until a "more convenient season," of weary, fruitless pilgrimages from one vague official to another, of long waits in government offices, of interminable delays and puttings-off, of prolonged correspondence with the powers that be, or were, in Constantinople—all such things as are best calculated to break the spirit of an eager American, to wear out his patience, dampen his ardor, and try to the uttermost his faith.

The first approach must be made to local officials. If by rare good fortune they are friendly, the application may slide through and a recommendation be sent on at once to the head Bureau of Education in Constantinople; but if, as is far more likely, they are time-serving individuals, whose sole interest is in their purses, the permission is a matter of months or years. They are fearful of offending local sentiment and making themselves unpopular, and they are equally fearful of jeopardizing their position with the government, so they take refuge in the evasions, prevarications, and subterfuges and postponements of which the Turk is past master.

With the petition must be presented the proposed curriculum, the names of the teachers, their diplomas, and also a statement of the house where the school is to be held. This of course necessitates leasing a house before the application for permission is made. If the permit is refused and the missionary is left with an expensive house on his hands for a year or more, it is a matter of no concern to his friend the Turk.

After a weary time the matter is settled locally, and the petition is passed on to Constantinople, with the recommendation that it be considered. Now it is necessary for the long-suffering missionary to communicate with the American Ambassador there, and request that the matter be followed up and the petition safely presented and not indefinitely shelved. More long delays, much writing and telegraphing to and fro, and in due season the missionary may, if he has fainted not, reap the reward of his long labors and receive his official irade to open a school.

Even then one may not be certain that the school will be forever free from the interference of the local authorities. Only a few weeks before the writing of this article, strong effort was made by the local Bureau of Education to prohibit the teaching of the Bible in the boys' school, doubtless at the instigation of some zealous citizens, in spite of the fact that such permission is specifically given in the Imperial irade. This attempt failing, they turned their attention to the girls' school and tried to find some flaw in its permit which would justify their closing it. Help came from an unexpected quarter. The authorities in Constantinople telegraphed to the Basrah officials that permissions which were once granted and recorded were unassailable, and that they desired to be troubled no further with complaints against the American schools in Basrah.

Having weathered this storm, the position of the educational work here should be stronger than ever, for, while the government has it in its power to cause many small annoyances and thwarting of plans, there can never again be the same struggle for existence and establishment.

A second part of this report dealt graphically with the difficulties encountered once the schools had begun:

The great initial difficulty overcome, of obtaining government permission, the would-be builders of schools find themselves confronted with other and more intangible difficulties. The ancient wall of Muslim tradition, prejudice, and distrust is a far more potent barrier than any technical one, and difference of race, creed, language, habit of thought and ethical standards make a high wall between Western teacher and Eastern parent and child. Especially is this true of the educational work for girls. The great women's movements of the present day are slow in making themselves felt in this backwater of the current of social progress, and the circumscribed life of the harem presents no obvious demand for any greater enlightenment, which would entail breaking the custom of centuries. An Oriental man may seek medical aid for himself and his family for their bodily ills, he may listen more or less courteously to an exposition of the alien faith, but he will think twice before entrusting his sons and daughters in the most plastic years of their lives to the daily training and influence of Christian teachers.

Competition in educational work exists in Basrah, but it is not a vital problem. The importance of the Koran schools and the small Muslim schools for girls is negligible, and the government boys' schools, although well equipped and subsidized, give all of their instruction in Turkish, and are so ill-managed and give such poor and unsystematic instruction that the boys emerge from them as ignorant as when they entered. The different sects of Eastern Christians maintain their own schools in Basrah—Chaldeans, Syrians, Armenians, and members of the Latin Church—as do the Jewish community, but these are primarily for the children of their own congregations, and not for Muslims. Diversity of language is a minor difficulty, not insuperable, as almost everyone understands Arabic, but still a hindrance. A class where one child's home langauge is Turkish, a second Persian, and a third Armenian, is harder to reach effectively in Arabic than through the children's mother tongue.

Arabic was the official language of both schools from the start, and was used for all the general branches. The boys' school had to offer Turkish and French, as they were the official languages of the Turkish Empire. English was in great demand because of the proximity to India. Then Persian had to be added because a group of influential boys with a Persian background came, bringing their own tutor with them. For a brief period five languages had to be fitted into the curriculum, resulting in a veritable Tower of Babel.

John secured as Turkish teacher the private secretary to the Governor's Council, who was half Turkish and half Arab and a good personal friend. Besides teaching Turkish, he passed on to John inside information about what was going on in the Council, especially as it might affect the school or the mission.

The Governor was a general in the Turkish army, so to please him as well as to benefit the boys, the astute principal asked for an officer of gendarmes to give military drill. His Excellency graciously sent an aide, who because of his association with the mission, and the added stipend which his teaching gave him, became very friendly and was a great "booster" for the school.

Despite opposition in the form of religious fanaticism and political suspicion, the School of High Hope grew. An increasing number of Arab fathers wanted modern education for their sons, and the school exactly suited them. Old-fashioned and zealous Muslim divines were alarmed and indignant at the growing popularity of this foreign institution, and the following protest was published in pamphlet form in Zobeir, a town near Basrah on the edge of the desert:

The Question

What say the wise of Islam, the benefit of God upon them, in particular and in general, of one whose religion is the religion of Islam, but who puts his child, male or female, into the schools of the Protestants, and they commissioned by the chiefs of their sect, to invite them to Christianity? For this they have their living with all necessities, and they spend what is needed to secure acceptance of their invitation, and they declare themselves to be teachers, together with the open assertion that they are missionaries, and among their wiles is companionship with doctors who care for the sick. They give free medicine to the poor to turn the hearts of the people to them, although the sick and those under instruction pray with them Christian prayers every day at the beginning and at the end of the day, and they clearly proclaim in their prayers the divinity of the Messiah and His Lordship, and they preach that there is no salvation except in the confident belief in that in which the Christians firmly believe. Is this permissible according to the law of Islam, or not permissible? We request a decision concerning this affliction, and to you be the blessing and the reward.

Praise be to God alone, and prayer and peace on Him than whom there is no prophet after Him.

The Reply

It is not permissible to one who believes in God and the last day, that he give over his child, male or female, to other teachers than Muslims, not in a school and not elsewhere, not even in the house of the Muslim himself, if there is even a suspicion of injury, to say nothing of certainty. And its certainty is a matter demonstrated. It is indeed a necessity recognized by all who possess discrimination and insight that the Muslim in these last years entrusts himself with no fears to the Abyssinian Christians, the Jews, the magicians and the idolaters, but it is not possible to entrust one's self without fear to the Christians from Europe and America, and especially these messengers of corruption who have no fruit except godlessness and apostasy. There is great danger in mixing with them, and danger to our families, and to our relatives and to our tribes, and to the government of our city; this to the point of the entrance of foreigners and their permanent establishment as has happened in most places of the Muslims. This is their root purpose, and their second purpose is to tear us away from our religion, that they may quiet all resistance if they wish to rule over us, because doubtless if there is no bond of religion we will separate, the one from the other, and our condition with them will be similar to the saying of orphans, "Whoever marries our mother he is our uncle." All who come to our country from Europe and America are servants of their governments, using every means to attain lordship over us. Their methods divide themselves into two procedures, which are united in the result, and one of them is our transformation from our religion to the religion of the Christians, and the second is to tear us away from all religion to worldly materialism, and in truth the first is a means to the second. The missionaries and all those with them, the doctors and the caretakers for the sick, and the people of the schools, are of the first method. And all the other doctors, not bound up with the missionaries, and all the travellers and the merchants and the people of the government are of the second method. Already the results of their works have appeared in most places of the Muslims, East and West, North and South, and this has increased their vigor, and the Muslims have not increased on this account, except in their decline. Therefore, whoever would surrender his boy or girl to these foreigners, he is lacking in that which distinguishes man from the beasts.

The prestige of the School of High Hope was greatly enhanced when Sheikh Khazal of Mohammerah sent his five sons, approximately the same age, all of different mothers. He was the ruler of the Province of Arabistan, over the Persian border, and was nominally under Persian suzerainty. The story went that when the Shah's emissary came down periodically from Teheran to collect the tribute due to his master, Sheikh Khazal paid him the money during the day, and won it all back playing poker at night. Khazal had treaty relations with Great Britain, and the British India ships always fired a salute as they passed his palace above Mohammerah, on their way up the Shatt-el-Arab river to Basrah. He was one of the persons considered as a possible emir for the new Kingdom of Iraq after World War I, before King Feisal the First was finally chosen.

Several Khazal grandsons came to school with their young uncles, and Hajji Rais, the Prime Minister of the Sheikh, sent sons and nephews, as did various lesser sheikhs. These boys, with their tutor, formed the nucleus of the boarding school which developed later. The great Sheikh Mobarek of Kuwait had advised his friend and protege, Khazal of Mohammerah, to send his boys to the School of High Hope, and several times when we took them home for vacations, Mobarek would be visiting Mohammerah. He would receive us ceremoniously on his yacht, and on one of these occasions he gave me a beautiful little enamelled watch set round with pearls, and expressed to me his appreciation of my care and concern for the boys. I got

The Rev. & Mrs. John Van Ess, Basrah, 1912, with boys at the boarding school from the family of Sheikh Khazal of Mohammerah.

acquainted with the mothers during these visits "down river," and learned to understand the factors in the domestic background which had such a powerful effect on the characters and reactions of their sons. This was of course very useful to my husband, who could never learn about it except through me.

The leading member of the powerful Naqib family, Sayyid Talib Pasha, also sent his sons to our school. As he was immensely influential throughout the whole region, his patronage and friendship caused the Turkish officials to slacken considerably their obstructive tactics.

In the meantime, my little school was becoming established. I had completed my language work, and opened the girls' school in the autumn of 1912. John made all arrangements for leasing premises and having them prepared. We secured a charming little house in Basrah City, near the one where the boys' school was already functioning, and furnished it attractively with modern school equipment from America. I even had a piano, a great rarity in those days and a tremendous drawing card. Notices were printed in Arabic and Turkish and circulated freely, and I hopefully awaited results. The only existing schools for Arab girls were the little Koran schools where the gabbling youngsters sat cross-legged on the floor, swaying to and fro as they learned the Holy Book by rote.

Several of my husband's Arab friends said to him, after our notices had begun to go around,

"Why in the world is your wife wasting her time and the mission's money by trying to have a school for Arab girls? Everyone knows you can't teach a female anything. A man might send his horse or his cow, or even his donkey to school, but a girl! Never!"

On the opening day it looked as though they might be right, for no one came; my teachers (one Christian Arab from Mardin and one Armenian who was to teach sewing and lace-work) both said:

"You see, it is hopeless! No Muslims will send their girls to school!"

On the second day one little Armenian girl came. The next day, the bright-eyed little daughters of the Persian consul appeared in gay silk dresses. Slowly the enrollment grew till we had about thirty little girls and were able to organize a real school.

We worked out a program which approximated the first four grades, as well as a kindergarten group. It was written into the Imperial charters of our schools that we were allowed to teach Bible daily, so from the beginning Christian teaching has been the foundation of our institutions.

Every morning in those early days, John and I set out together in our bellum, poled by two muscular boatmen. At that time practically all transportation was by boat, on the canals and on the river. Large country boats called mahalas conveyed all the freight and fuel, and gaily painted bellums the passenger traffic, with neat white awnings to shield passengers from the summer sun. Small black canoes, mesh-hufs, darted through the busy creek traffic like water beetles, skillfully piloted by Ma'adan Arab women from the marshes taking their dairy products to market. The ride from our house along the winding creek to Basrah City took about half an hour and was absorbingly interesting. It is by far the most comfortable and glamorous "commuting" I have ever done.

John often took an Arabic newspaper with him in the boat and would regale me with the high spots of the news as we glided along. Sometimes he would have an Arabic magazine from Cairo of a very high literary quality which he compared to the Atlantic Monthly. He kept himself up to the mark in Arabic by watching to see if he could read one page of this as rapidly as its equivalent in English. Some of this rubbed off painlessly on me, and as we passed a rosy clump of oleanders in full bloom my husband would teach me a new and erudite Arabic word.

We took our lunch in a large wicker "tiffin basket" and at the noon recess when the last little Fatima had donned her black abba and tripped home to her dinner my husband would come over from the nearby boys' school and we would have our luncheon together in my office. We would exchange news, particularly anything that affected me and my work.

My old Arab janitress, Om Jasm (the Mother of Jasm), made us tea in a samovar down in the courtyard and brought it up to us in steaming glasses as we ate our sandwiches. She clucked over us like a motherly hen and would run up and down the stairway on a dozen needless errands to add to our comfort and well-being.

"I have a message for you from the father of one of your girls," said John one day, as he was finishing off his meal with dates.

"Fozi Mahmoud wants you to teach Fozie more and faster and he will pay you higher fees."

I groaned. Fozie was a particularly dull girl.

"You know," observed my husband reflectively, "these parents think that human minds are like a cup, to be filled from the pitcher of knowledge. It all depends on how fast the hand that holds the pitcher pours it out."

Sometime after New Year's John remarked to me, as we were enjoying our walnut cookies,

"I wish you could find out what has happened to Ali Shakir to make him slump in his studies. He used to be one of the best students in the upper school but just lately he seems to have lost all interest. He doesn't study and has a bad attitude toward his teachers. He won't talk to any of us. It isn't like him at all."

"Well," I replied, "I think I know where he lives because one of my little girls is his cousin and I believe the families live in the same courtyard. I'll try to go there this afternoon."

When I arrived at Ali's house I was heartily welcomed by a large group of family and friends crowded into a little reception room. The center of interest was a gaudily clad young girl of not more than thirteen: she was dripping with jewelry and sat with downcast eyes on a gay cushion.

Ali's father had just married a new wife.

After conveying my somewhat hollow congratulations and good wishes to the bride I sought out Ali's mother in a distant room.

"He took her on my head," exclaimed Ali's mother bitterly. (This expression is commonly used when a man adds another wife to his family. Islam allows four legal wives. A wealthy man usually provides each spouse with a separate establishment, which makes for peace. When all four live together there is occasion for jealousy and strife.)

"Haven't I given him sons? Haven't I slaved all these years looking after him and his children? But no! That isn't enough! He must have a young fresh plaything. He has dyed his beard and bought himself all new clothes."

She looked sharply at me.

"*You* haven't brought any sons yet, but your husband wouldn't take another wife on your head, would he?"

I assented and confirmed the fact that Christians have only one wife.

"It is fate!" she exclaimed with the inevitable fatalism of Islam. "God is great!"

Ali was deeply devoted to his mother and I had the answer for John. His prize pupil was undergoing such a profound emotional upset that he could think of nothing else for the time being.

Over another lunch during this halcyon period John remarked as he peeled me a succulent Baquba orange,

"Mullah Cassim came in to see me this morning on business that concerns both you and me."

"And what might that be?"

"He wants me to excuse Hussein from Bible classes and you to do the same for Khadijah."

"What did you tell him?" I asked, knowing quite well what the answer would be.

"I said that no Muslim children were obliged to come to our schools but that they seek us out and not we them—that we charge fees and that the condition on which we accept pupils is that they conform to our program.

"I also added for good measure that the official permits for our schools were signed by the Sultan of Turkey and who was Mullah Cassim to set himself up against the Caliph of all Believers?"

The man had been somewhat deflated. His answer was,

"The moral atmosphere in your schools and your character training are so good that we like our children to be with you. There is just this matter of the difference in religion."

John admonished him,

"Don't you realize that it is because our schools are founded on Christian principles that the atmosphere is good?"

One noon my husband strode gleefully into my little office and as he surveyed our attractive lunch set out on gaily flowered plates from the bazaar he observed,

"Well, there are a few of my boys who aren't going to enjoy their noon meal today as much as you and I will!"

He went on to say that he had instituted a new punishment for foul language or lying.

"I told the boys that the tongue was sick and needed medicine," he explained with gusto:

So I stood up the offenders, about ten of them, before the whole school and made them open their mouths wide and then put on the back of the tongue of each boy in turn a good big dose of powered quinine. They all rushed off to drink water but this just intensified the bitter taste. It will last about an hour. And the beauty of it is that the quinine is good for them because most of these boys are full of malaria.

I was charmed with this idea where so aptly "the punishment fit the crime" and used it successfully all the rest of my teaching days.

I was very strict about maintaining my official seclusion and trained my old "Om Jasm" to be a real dragon as a door-keeper. If anyone masculine came to the door, even a messenger from the Director of Education with a communication bristling with imposing seals, she would shoo him away with a shocked, "No, no, you can't come in here. This is a *girls'* school! Take it to the principal of the boys' school over yonder. He is the *Khanum's* husband and he will give it to her at the proper time."

The Turks couldn't raise any objection to this as it was a leaf out of their own book, and my rigid observance of their system, which kept all but the smallest girls in seclusion, was highly approved by the parents of my Muslim girls. We frequently employed other delaying tactics learned from the Turks in a most useful manner.

I had a weekly "At Home" in the girls' school. The whole town was curious and interested and flocked to see our setup. Many of the mothers of school-boys used to come not only to make my acquaintance, but to ask me to convey some special request or complaint or comment to my husband or to put in a good word from their sons with the teachers. Sometimes I got the credit for a favor that would have been granted anyway, which enhanced my prestige and did no one any harm. By coming to Basrah as the wife of a man who was known, trusted, and liked, I had a ready-made place, which was an immense advantage as I began the girls' school.

Every afternoon I went calling, trying to visit the families of all my girls in turn, and as many of the boys' homes as possible: from the imposing pillared palace of the sheikh, set among fertile reaches of date gardens on the river front; to the city mansion of the pasha with its glittering chandeliers, gaudy ornaments, and priceless carpets; from the comfortable old-fashioned Arab house of a well-to-do landowner, where the charcoal brazier and a steaming samovar gave a cheery welcome to guests on crisp winter afternoons; to the courtyard of a Mullaya (a woman religious leader), hung with black for a Shiah Muslim reading; on to the houses of army officers, clerks in government offices, carpenters, policemen and shopkeepers. To any family daring enough to send their children to an American mission school I found my way, received a most cordial welcome, and experienced a varied and fascinating slice of life.

By the second year, the girls' school had outgrown the pleasant little house where we had begun, and we had to rent a larger one. Our numbers increased slowly but steadily, and girls from leading Arab families became my pupils. Three of these, who were eager and intelligent, and making excellent progress, one day failed to appear.

"Their father says they are too old to go to school," volunteered a neighbor. (They were perhaps nine, eleven and twelve years old.)

"Would it do any good if I went to their house and talked with their mothers?" I inquired hopefully. (They were the children of partner wives.)

"I don't think so," was the discouraging answer, "whatever the father says, must be."

I did go, but to no avail, and later on I received what was

intended for a consoling message from our friend Sayyid Talib Pasha.

"Say to Mrs. Van Ess—what does the father know, that the daughters should know anything?"

We put on one impressive play in this early period, when any kind of entertainment for women was a rarity. It was a drama of Queen Esther and King Ahasuerus, as lavishly staged and costumed as our resources, and the girls' family wardrobes, could achieve. The courtyard and upper verandahs were packed, not only with the invited guests but with many gatecrashers, eager to see this unusual spectacle. They all followed the plot with breathless interest and voluble comments. One old lady asked in a loud voice,

"This king—is it George or Edward?"

I think she was the same dowager who once asked me if I spoke "Protestani." This useful adjective was applied to everything pertaining to us, especially the mission hospital, though our schools were usually referred to as the "American."

A fellow guest at a large "At Home" of Arab ladies once asked me if I knew English.

The first period of our schools under the rule of the old Ottoman Empire was drawing to a close faster than we knew. Our initial struggle against religious fanaticism was over. The prejudice against girls' education was breaking down.

We were well established and occupied a unique position as the only modern schools in the whole region conducted in the Arabic language.

We were ready for whatever the future might hold.

VIII

The End of an Era

The winds of change had been blowing over the old Ottoman Empire for some time before the fatal day in October, 1914, when Turkey entered the First World War on the side of Germany against Britain and her allies.

Britain had been the friend of Turkey for many years and had tried to preserve the solidity of the crumbling Empire. Much of its domains in what was called Asiatic Turkey were Arab countries, whose bond with Turkey was the religion of Islam. The Sultan was the Caliph of all believers, the Defender of the Faith, and the Protector of the Holy Cities, Mecca and Medina in the Hejaz—the goal of pilgrimage for Muslims all over the world. As long as this relationship held the Arab world was firmly bound to Turkey. The position deteriorated during the latter years of Sultan Abdul Hamid's reign, and still more when the Young Turk party came into power and began its ruthless Pan-Turanian policy. After the Balkan wars of 1912 and 1913, when nearly all of European Turkey was lost, a new Turkish nationalism showed itself to be strongly anti-Arab and even anti-Muslim. As the Turkish army was being imbued with this sentiment, the relations between Arab and Turkish army officers became very strained.

Britain still tried to help maintain Ottoman integrity. In June, 1913, Sir Edward Gray wrote to the British Ambassador in Berlin:

Respecting Asiatic Turkey, I had observed that there were two possible courses. One was to consolidate the remaining Turkish dominions and to put Turkey on her feet. The other course was a division of Asiatic Turkey into spheres of interest. This would lead to partition and the complete disappearance of the Turkish Empire.

In July, 1913, Sir Edward Gray wrote to the British ambassador in Constantinople:

A grave policy is involved and the only policy to which we

can become a party is one directed to avoid collapse and
partition of Asiatic Turkey. The effect of the opposite course
upon our own Mussalmans in India would be disastrous, to say
nothing of the complications that would be produced between
European powers.

In the meantime Germany was assiduously cultivating Turkey
and seeking her goodwill. At a time when other powers were
critical of the Turks because of the Armenian massacres, this
attitude was especially appreciated. The German emperor had
paid a visit to the Holy Land, and in Jerusalem had proclaimed
himself as "Hajji Wilhelm," friend and champion of the Muslims. German military officers were training and equipping the
Turkish army. Of course Germany had her eye on the proposed
Berlin to Baghdad Railway, which would have to pass through
Asiatic Turkey. We discovered after the outbreak of war that
most of the young Germans in the firm of Robert Wonckhouse
and Company were reserve army officers. They had a large
office in Basrah and other branches in various ports down the
Gulf. They studied Arabic, made friends with the local population, and were extremely liberal in their business dealings with
Arab merchants.

During the summer of 1914 the atmosphere in Basrah became increasingly tense. In May the British consul, Mr. Crow,
had gone on leave and his place was taken by R. W. Bullard
(now Sir Reader Bullard) of the Levant service. We became
friends at once and shared together the anxieties of that critical
period. During the summer vacation John and I went to live in
one of Sheikh Khazal's Basrah "palaces," directly on the river.
Across from us was anchored for many weeks a German merchant ship whose captain and officers were very friendly. They
came often to call and were very generous with gifts of ham,
sausages, and other delicacies from their stores. After war between Germany and Britain had been declared in August, 1914,
they continued to come often to see us and enjoyed discussing
the war with my husband, who spoke fluent German. I was
always nervous for fear they might call when Mr. Bullard was
staying with us, as he did most weekends, or when some of our
other British friends had dropped in for a cold drink on our
pleasant balcony overlooking the river. Fortunately such a situation never occurred.

The general sentiment in Basrah at that time was pro-German. All the leading officials were of course Turks, whose sympathies were with the anti-Entente policy of the Cabinet in Constantinople and with the Sultan who as Caliph had declared a Holy War—a Jehad. All the official news circulated to the general public made much of the losses of Britain and her allies and of their difficulties and predicted a speedy German victory.

The Young Turk party abolished the "Capitulations," a long-standing agreement by which foreigners residing in Turkey were not subject to Ottoman jurisdiction but could be prosecuted only through their own consuls. This meant in Basrah that the British Post Office (which we all used) was closed and that foreigners could be arrested directly on the slightest charge.

The local gendarmes and soldiers became increasingly insolent and disrespectful to Europeans. I well remember one afternoon when John and I had been to tea with Mr. Bullard at the British Consulate, and he walked out with us to his pier on the river where our bellum was waiting to take us home. A Turkish soldier, one of the regular guard of the Consulate, was half sitting and half lying on the river bank, and instead of springing to his feet and saluting as he should have done, he remained in his lounging position and regarded the British consul through half-closed eyes.

"I'd like to kick him into the river!" exclaimed John wrathfully after we had passed him.

"Never mind," said Reader Bullard soothingly. "His time will come!"

An old light-ship was towed down the river and sunk in the channel, but before this happened, all the British merchant ships, waiting to load dates, had left the harbor. They had been warned to do so in a telegram from their Embassy in Constantinople. Later on the German ship, whose officers had been so friendly to us, was also sunk in the channel by orders from Turkish officials to its reluctant and regretful captain. (These sunken vessels shifted their position with the changing tides and currents and were never the obstacle intended.)

One day late in October we were expecting Mr. Bullard to tea and dinner, when we received a note from him asking us to come to him instead, as he could not leave his compound. We were somewhat mystified, and still more so when we reached the Consulate and found him in the most uproarious high spirits. It was obvious that he had received some official good news which he had to keep secret. I can still see him sitting at the piano in the huge Consulate drawing room, playing and singing with immense gusto the Negro spiritual which ends,

"It must be now de Kingdom coming, and de year of Jubilo!"

He informed us cheerfully that he could not leave his premises, and that we must come to him, which we did nearly every day till the end of the month. On October 30, 1914, war was declared between Turkey and Britain. The British consul then collected those of his community who were still in Basrah (many Englishmen, not essential to their firms, had left and joined up) and escorted them to the paddle-wheel steamer which was waiting to take them down the river to Persian waters. At the last moment, in spite of earlier promises to the contrary, the acting Turkish governor allowed no one to go except the consul. (The others spent the next three weeks very comfortably under house arrest in their own homes.) Mr. Bullard offered to take with him the women of our mission—myself, Mrs. Bennett and her little boy, and Miss Wilhelmina Holzhauser, the R.N. who was the superintendent of our hospital—but we declined with grateful thanks.

We then learned that the good news of "Kingdom Coming" which Reader Bullard had longed to tell us earlier, was that a British Expeditionary Force had been concentrated at Bahrain, halfway down the Persian Gulf, as soon as it seemed inevitable that Turkey was about to declare war against Britain. This was Indian Expeditionary Force "D" (IEFD) which was to play a leading part in the Mesopotamian campaign.

In September a minute had been written by Sir Edmund Barron, military secretary of the India office, on "The role of India in a Turkish War." Its conclusion was:

This seems the psychological moment to take action. So unexpected a stroke at this moment would have a startling effect:

(1) It would checkmate Turkish intrigues and demonstrate our ability to strike.

(2) It would encourage the Arabs to rally to us and confirm the Sheikhs of Mohammerah and Kuwait in their allegiance.

(3) It would safeguard Egypt, and without Arab support a Turkish invasion is impossible.

(4) It would effectually protect the oil installations at Abadan.

Such results seem to justify fully the proposed action.

The first point referred, among other possibilities, to the fear that Turkish and German agents might try to go through Iraq to Afghanistan and India. There were rumors that the Germans might establish a submarine base at Fao, at the mouth of the river; and that Turkish troops had been seen going south, which implied that an attack on Kuwait was contemplated.

On October 31, Lord Kitchener sent an historic cable to Emir Abdullah, second son of King Hussein of the Hejaz, who had already been conferring with British officials in Cairo about Arab dissatisfaction with Turkish rule. It read:

Salaams to Sherif Abdullah. Germany has now bought the Turkish Government with gold, notwithstanding that England, France and Russia guaranteed integrity of Ottoman Empire if Turkey remained neutral in the War. Turkish Government have against will of Sultan committed acts of aggression by invading the frontiers of Egypt with bands of Turkish soldiers. If Arab nation assists England in this war England will guarantee that no intervention takes place in Arabia and will give Arabs every assistance against external foreign aggression.

The day that Basrah received the news of Turkey's entry into the war, twelve leading Arabs of the region came to call on John. They were also Turkish army officers and were in full uniform. They sat in his study, gravely discussing with him all the aspects of the international situation. Several of them indicated to him that they would fight against Turkey if it would lead to Arab independence. Within a few months they were all doing so. A few days later the five paramount Arab sheikhs of the region also met in my husband's study. With his help and advice they worked out a statement of support for the Allied side, which was to be of greatest value to the British forces, and a serious loss to the Turkish side, which had counted on help from local tribes in southern Iraq.

It was now, for the only time in his life, that John held a government post. He was asked by Ambassador Henry Morgan-thau in Constantinople to act as American consul in Basrah. This is quite against mission rules and procedures, but cabled permission was promptly given by our headquarters in New York, which recognized the emergency and the urgency of the situation. Thereupon followed a most uneasy three weeks. All sorts of rumors were flying around, and we felt terribly cut off from authentic news of how the war was going. Fortunately, and to us amazingly, our schools continued in their normal way. The British were already attacking Fao, sixty miles down the river; our city was full of soldiers; Holy War mobs shouted and surged through the streets. Even though bullets were whistling, John's boys and my girls still came to school.

Then finally, one morning early, our servant came to our bedroom door before we were up, and said in an awe-struck voice,

"Sahib, sellemou!"

Literally this means, "They've surrendered!" but in this case it meant "They've evacuated."

We looked out the window to the little police post next door which had been such a center of activity, and sure enough it was empty. The Turkish army, in full retreat from the south after the British had captured Fao, had decided not to try to hold Basrah, but had moved northward in a desperate attempt to establish a firm base from which it would be easier to resist the British forces. All senior government officials, taking most of their essential records, went with the army. Not even a skeleton police force was left to maintain law and order.

An incredible period of anarchy followed, with looting and plundering and indiscriminate killing. The Custom House was the richest source of booty, and bales of cloth and silk and velvet and every other sort of goods were seized and carried off. One hapless garry-driver was shot and killed for the sake of three bars of soap, which he had on his lap as he whipped up his galloping horses in a vain attempt to escape. Doors and window-frames of government buildings were torn out and carried off, as well as the furniture and any available papers.

Our house and the boys' school, now next door, were guarded by deserting Turkish soldiers who took refuge with us after the retreat. They were Christian Arabs who had been unwillingly conscripted at the outbreak of war and they were only too glad to leave the army and join forces with us. They looked extremely fierce as they patrolled our roofs, with their Turkish rifles and drawn bayonets, and they worked out a schedule for night and day duty, as they did for our hospital compound and everyone there.

A minor Turkish official brought his entire family and

dumped them in our boarding-school for safety—two wives, an old grandmother, and an assortment of children. He came back and collected them some days later, when the British had occupied Basrah and order was restored.

During this time of anarchy, we had the temerity to go down to our hospital compound every day dodging flying bullets. We wore conspicuous Red Crescent arm-bands (in Muslim countries the equivalent of the Red Cross), and were closely escorted by one of our ex-soldier guards. The hospital was overflowing with casualties from the disastrous Turkish retreat, and the Doctors Bennett and Miss Holzhauser were only too thankful to have extra help with rolling bandages, preparing dressings, and doing any odd jobs that came to hand.

After what seemed an incredible delay, with lawlessness in town increasing at an alarming rate, John realized that it was possible that the British did not know that the Turks had evacuated Basrah. Accordingly, in his capacity as acting American consul, he wrote a letter addressed to the general commanding the British forces, telling him of the situation and urging him to send a token force as soon as possible to restore order. He sent it down river at night by one of our most intrepid boatmen, who used his "protective coloring" to make his way safely to British headquarters and deliver his message. (This letter is now in the National Archives in Washington.)

H.M.S. "Espiegle" was sent up the river at once, and fired a cannon as soon as it reached the Custom House at the corner of Ashar Creek. Instantly all the scattered firing, which had been continuous and increasing for several days, ceased, and a death-like silence prevailed.

Town criers were then sent all over the city, announcing in Arabic:

"The Man-of-War says" (we liked the idea of H.M.S. "Espiegle" opening its mouth and declaiming) "that all shooting must stop, everyone shall stay in house until order is restored, and a regular military government will be set up at once."

The proclamation implied that there would be no reprisals, that normal life would be resumed immediately, and that law-abiding citizens need have no fear.

Next morning bright and early John and I set out in our bellum, flying the American flag. We surmised that the British General Headquarters would be set up in the British Consulate, and John knew that they would wish to get in touch with him at once. We were thrilled to see the Union Jack flying on the flag-pole at the mouth of the creek instead of the Star and Crescent, and still more thrilled when a British Tommy standing on the bank, remarked admiringly as he saw the Stars and Stripes fluttering from our bellum,

"'ansome flag that!"

IX
The Mission and the First World War

As soon as the British General Headquarters was established in Basrah in November, 1914, the general commanding officer appointed a military governor with two deputies, and our friend Reader Bullard as civil advisor. He had come back with the first British contingent, and was invaluable with his knowledge of Basrah and of the departed Turks. Sir Percy Cox, who had served many years in the Persian Gulf area, and was the head political resident at the outbreak of war, was the chief political officer for the new regime in Iraq, and was political adviser to the army commander. He was responsible for the civil administration which had to be set up at once. All the senior Turkish officials had fled with the army, and their posts had to be filled by British political officers, who consulted constantly with the military authorities. Local officials were rounded up and many returned to their jobs, though a little fearful as to what might happen to them if the Turks some day returned. The general public soon settled down and accepted the new state of affairs. There was plenty of employment, due to the presence of the occupying army and its needs, and an unaccustomed prosperity reached down even to the poorest stratum of society.

John overheard one Arab say to another,

"The Turks, the peace of God be upon them, were very hard on us, but these British, God curse them for unbelievers, they do treat you well."

Our schools reopened after being closed only about eight days during the Turkish retreat and evacuation and the succeeding days of anarchy. The boys' school now had an important part to play in the new regime, for Arab personnel were desperately needed by the new administration, and there were few Arabs with enough education to qualify. The army needed interpreters, and a knowledge of English was at a premium. The students who had been in the School of High Hope were in great demand, and fresh applicants for admission flocked to its doors.

John was constantly consulted by the British from that first morning onwards. Sir Percy Cox interrogated him about the probable number of the Turkish forces, of their conduct and attitude (which had been admirable) during the three weeks before they evacuated Basrah, and what their possible plans might be. He also questioned us closely about the sentiments of the local population, and what their attitude was likely to be under British occupation.

A reliable police force was one of the first necessities for Basrah, and the American missionary had contacts with the Arabs which enabled him to select men who could be trusted, and who had the ability to do the job. He even designed their uniforms.

He also picked several of the secret agents who went back and forth behind the Turkish lines at great personal risk, and brought back valuable information. Some of them preferred to communicate it through him, and he would relay it to the authorities.

One night John had a secret visit from a tribal sheikh who controlled twelve thousand Arabs.

"The Turks have offered me $125,000 if we will join them," he confided. "If the British will give me $200,000 we will go with them and refuse the Turks."

My husband accordingly passed the news to the British commander, who rejected the offer with some indignation. (Afterwards, we knew that on the other side of Arabia, Lawrence was distributing British gold to the Arabs with a lavish hand.)

The next night the sheikh came in quietly for his answer. When he heard of the refusal he remarked,

"I am sorry. I think the British are going to win, and I would like to be on the winning side."

With a shrug of his shoulders he departed, and the next day took his men to the Turks.

Our friend Sayyid Talib Pasha el Naqib made advances to the British after the outbreak of war, through another of our friends—the Sheikh of Mohammerah. He said that if he were given authority to do so he would raise an Arab revolt. Sheikh Khazal advised him to co-operate with him and Sheikh Mobarek of Kuwait and Ibn Saud—the latter already a figure rising on the Arab horizon. Talib might claim the hereditary privileges of the Naqebs, of immunity from taxes, and hope to escape Turkish reprisals. He went to Kuwait and then to Ibn Saud. (After that he went to India where he remained until 1917, when he went to Egypt.)

Our mission hospital continued to serve all comers. A contingent of Turkish officers who were in a camp across the river when the British occupied Basrah were taken prisoner, and some of them were ill and were brought to our hospital by the British authorities. John used to visit them often, and there was one young officer with whom he became especially friendly. He was completely out of spending money and asked my husband to lend him a gold Turkish pound. John did so willingly, and never allowed him to pay it back—for the young officer was Nuri Pasha Said, a leading Arab nationalist and many times in the future to be Prime Minister of Iraq.

"I like to feel that the prime minister of this country owes me money!" John used to declare whenever Nuri Pasha tried to pay his debt.

I had my own small part to play in the readjustments of those early days. The new civil administration knew that there were a good many families in Basrah who had received pensions from the Turkish Government. These were petty officials who had retired, or widows of men who had been in the Ottoman Civil Service. All the records pertaining to pensions had been taken away or destroyed, so the British political administrator summoned the Mukhtar, or head man, of each of the small districts within the municipality of Basrah. They were told to prepare lists of the people in their districts who had received Turkish pensions, as presumably these were administered through the Mukhtars. Lists were duly submitted, and the political officer who received them very wisely decided that if it were possible they should be investigated.

I was approached and asked if I could undertake such an investigation. I knew Arabic, I had the welfare of the poor people of Basrah at heart, and although I was officially neutral, I did not wish to see the British Government exploited by unscrupulous persons. My school was running very successfully, but I had always arranged the program so that I could be free in the afternoons when necessary.

For several weeks I went every afternoon to one or another of the little districts, where I looked up the Mukhtar and checked every person on his recommended list. I had with me one of our "Bible Women," a Christian Arab with a wide acquaintance all over Basrah and its outskirts. She was middle-aged and experienced, kindly but exceedingly shrewd, and woe betide anyone who tried to deceive her with a trumped-up hard luck story. We exposed several frauds—friends or relatives of the Mukhtars, who thought it was worthwhile to try to get in on the "gravy train"; and we had one amusing experience of the opposite nature. A family on our list were profoundly and vocally indignant that they should be considered an object of charity, much less British charity.

"Indeed we never had any money from the Turks, and we don't want any from the 'Engleze' (English). We are Arabs and we have enough property to support ourselves," declared the spokesman angrily.

They then poured the vials of their wrath on the head of the luckless Mukhtar who had included their names, no doubt hoping to win their favor. On the whole, most of the names submitted were bona fide claimants, and it was satisfying to know that deserving people were helped. The whole project created goodwill for everyone concerned.

We had a double company of soldiers quartered close to us, and became very friendly with the various officers as they came and went. At Christmas time I had my cook make a large frosted cake and sent it to the non-commissioned officers and the British Tommies. The sergeant brought back the clean plate the next day with appropriate thanks, and my husband invited him in for a chat.

"What do you think of the way the war is going, sergeant?" he inquired hospitably.

"Well, sir," replied the man, who was sitting stiffly on the edge of his chair, "I think the thing to do is to catch the 'Kayser'."

"How would you go about it?" asked John.

"Well sir, begging your pardon sir, that's for them to say as has the saying of it," was the reply, which became a classic among our friends.

One of John's main contributions to the war effort was his grammar, *Spoken Arabic of Mesopotamia*. He produced it at amazing speed at the request of the British military government, for the benefit of officers who wanted to get a working knowledge of Arabic as soon as possible. For this reason, he had to use transliteration into English characters, alongside the Arabic script, a procedure which pained him deeply. He had an Arabic typewriter, as well as his English one, and he put in the Arabic vowels in the text himself, by hand, for the copy which was to be sent to Oxford for publication. (His Arabic typewriter had only the consonants on its keyboard.) The clerk in Sir Arnold Wilson's office, in the political section, was supposed to mail it to catch a certain ship. He failed to do so, and was duly reprimanded, so it went in the following convoy. The ship which the clerk's negligence missed was sunk by an enemy submarine. A story without a moral.

The first consignment of printed grammars *was* in a ship sunk by enemy action on its way to the Near East. It had to be replaced, which was costly but easily accomplished, as the type was still set up. Professor Margoliuth of Oxford, a renowned Semitic scholar, saw the grammar through the press. John used to teach classes in Arabic, in what was called the "Khaki University" in Basrah, and also acted as examiner. For those coming up for the Field Test, he was told, "Pass them if you can." There was a financial bonus to anyone who succeeded. The Higher Proficiency examination earned a much higher bonus, and his instructions concerning that were, "Pass them if you must!"

He wrote a second book called *Practical Written Arabic*, which he considered a much better piece of work than the first from a scholarly standpoint.

However, *Spoken Arabic of Iraq*, as it is now called, has become standard. It has been through many reprintings and a second edition, and is still in print. Whenever I am in Oxford, I take pleasure in going into the bookshop of the Oxford University Press, going to the corner marked "Foreign Grammars," and seeing my husband's book on the shelf. It is used by the oil companies for their staff, and by other business and government concerns. I have been told that one young Englishman in Baghdad asked another,

"Have you Van Ess'd yet?"

For years the royalties have gone into a scholarship fund in the School of High Hope in Basrah. The vocabulary of the second edition was reprinted by the American Government during the Second World War, and circulated among American servicemen who were serving in Arabic-speaking areas.

Another service which the Mission did for the British administration in Basrah was to organize a school system. After the

Turks left, the School of High Hope was the only school for Arab boys in the whole region. The British Commander, Sir John Nixon, was keenly aware of the need of providing for education in the occupied territories, and he asked my husband to undertake the task of setting up a school system. The chief difficulty was to secure teachers. All the Turkish schoolmasters had departed, and most of them didn't know Arabic anyway. However John knew the region and the people, and finally was able to recruit a number of young men from the Arab population. Some of them were taken from prison ships and concentration camps. These had held minor positions under the Turkish government, and were technically enemies. They were only too pleased to renounce their former allegiance and promise good behavior under British military occupation. In due time four schools were equipped and operating.

Actually it was I who opened the first government school in Iraq. In the autumn of 1915 John had everything nearly ready, and the last touches were to be put on the house secured for a school while he was away at Bahrain at our annual mission meeting. The school was in Abul Khassib, a prosperous suburb of Basrah among the date gardens about ten miles down the river. He expected to be gone about ten days, if the normal schedule of British India ships had been maintained. To our consternation the regular "fast mail" was commandeered to bring troops from India, and week after week the passenger service was cancelled. This was during the melancholy period when a Turkish counterattack had driven the British forces in retreat back down the river to Kut el Amarsh, after an attempt to capture Baghdad.

Bahrain had no cable or wireless at that time, and John and his colleagues, impatiently waiting for a ship, had no idea what was happening.

In Basrah, I knew only too well what was happening, but was fortunately so run off my feet with work that I had no time to pine. I was the only missionary in the station, as the Cantines were on furlough in America; the Bennetts had been on vacation in India, and were attending mission meeting in Bahrain on the way home to Basrah. I was running my own school and supervising the boys' school, including the boarding department. The lively sons of Sheikh Khazal nearly set fire to the house one cold night, and one of them fell ill with what looked like diphtheria but fortunately wasn't.

During this hectic period, the young Arab whom John had secured to be headmaster for the first government school came to me and said,

"Mrs. Van Ess, everything is ready for that new school to begin, and the Abul Khassib boys are impatient to start. Must we wait for Mr. Van Ess to return?"

To which I replied,

"Certainly not, let's begin! Go ahead and open the school!"

In after years, Tahir Effendi rose to be the head of an important government department in the independent Kingdom of Iraq, and whenever he and I met we would say to each other,

"*We* began the government schools in Iraq!"

The end of the month came around and all the hospital staff came to me, wanting to have their salaries paid. The Bennetts had expected to be back long before the end of November, and all their hospital books were with them in Bahrain for the annual mission audit. I had no idea what the details of their budget were. Luckily John had left me a very large bank balance in our joint checking account, and I was able to give everybody something. In desperation I kept a day-book which I posted up each night, staying up late in the attempt to keep my multitudinous accounts in some sort of order, but it took my poor husband the rest of the winter to get it all sorted out.

One vivid memory I have, among many of those harried weeks, is of a morning when I had to go to school by horsegarry because the tide was too low for the bellum. As the driver started his horses, five people ran alongside the carriage shouting messages at me—a carpenter, a servant from the boarding school, someone from the hospital and someone from the Bible shop, and one of my own domestic staff.

I have never forgotten Lady Cox's kindness to me during those weeks when I was alone. Sir Percy Cox had established his wife in the Cantines' house during their absence, down the road from me. She had urged me to come and stay with her, but since that was impossible she had me to as many meals as I could spare time for, and kept in touch with me daily to make sure I was all right.

Another indelible recollection is the relentless punctuality of a high school student who came every afternoon at 4:30 all those weeks, for special instruction in English. He was a diligent and earnest young man from Shuster, in Sheikh Khazal's territory, who needed extra tutoring to catch up with an advanced class. John had asked me before he left if I could continue coaching Mustafa for the "week or ten days" he would be absent. I had assented cheerfully, and told the youth to come every afternoon as soon as I was back from the girls' school in Basrah City. My reward for this work of supererogation was that it was my faithful Mustafa who told me, just before Christmas, of the probable arrival of a merchant steamship of the Bombay-Persian line. He said confidently,

"The agents here have told me it would surely stop in Bahrain, and it will be here any day now. I am certain that Mr. Van Ess will be on it!"—and so he was.

It was pleasant to have Major Bullard, as he was now, in Basrah all this time. Another good friend of the winter of 1915–1916 was Mrs. D. L. R. Lorimer, the wife of an officer in the Indian Political. He was on his way to Kerman, in Persia, but because the road was unsafe could not go there at once, and was assigned to temporary duty in the civil administration in Iraq. He and Major Bullard proceeded up the river, and Mrs. Lorimer stayed in Basrah and acted as editor of the *Basrah Times*, the army newspaper, till such time as the road to Kerman should be opened. She was a gifted and brilliant woman, a philologist of note (as was her husband) and had been a don at Somerville—one of the women's colleges at Oxford. The little newspaper flourished under her leadership. We greatly enjoyed her companionship and had much in common. She and I achieved a brief notoriety among the townspeople because once after heavy winter rains, when mud made the roads impassable for traffic, we donned rubber boots and walked from our houses in Ashar to our respective places of work in Basrah City—she to the office of the *Basrah Times* and I to my school. I found only one teacher, and three or four girls, but the moral effect was tremendous.

This was a dreary winter with the siege of the Kut garrison heavily on our minds and hearts. Repeated attempts to relieve them were unsuccessful, as the Turkish resistance was unexpectedly strong, and in April the gallant British force had to surrender, was taken prisoner, and marched away across Asiatic Turkey.

In March tragedy befell our mission. Our hospital had been caring for wounded soldiers since the outbreak of the war. The medical facilities of the British "IEFD" (Indian Expeditionary

Force) were woefully inadequate, in fact the conditions under which the wounded were sent down the river to the base became a matter eventually of parliamentary investigation of the "Mesopotamian Scandal." We were in any case better equipped than they to deal with sick and wounded Turkish prisoners, and in March a contingent was sent to us, suffering from what proved to be typhus fever. This is highly infectious, and soon almost every member of our hospital staff succumbed to it. Several local employees died, and many of the prisoners. Miss Holzhauser, our Nursing Superintendent, had it so severely that she was later invalided home to America, never to be able to return. Finally both Dr. and Mrs. Bennett came down with the dread disease. By that time it had been identified, and they were both removed to the infectious section of Basrah General Hospital. Ironically, this was centered in the very Khazal palace where John and I had lived so happily during the fateful summer of 1914.

Christine Bennett had a short severe attack and in a few days died. The loss of the friend and companion whose life had been so close to mine was a very deep sorrow. It was made all the more poignant because I had been taking care of three-year-old Matthew Bennett, and I had to tell him that his mother was dead. When I came back from her funeral, I took him on my lap and told him that his mother was all well now, but that God had had to take her to Heaven to make her so. He looked up at me trustingly and said,

"Isn't there a way down from there?"

I explained as best I could, and he accepted it; and I knew that he had understood because he repeated it all very sweetly in Arabic to an Arab Christian family, where I often sent him with his nurse to play with their children.

All Basrah mourned with us. Arab women especially paid their tribute to Christine's selfless devotion in serving them and their children with her medical skill. Their grief was profound and sincere. The whole community was drawn together and to us in their sense of loss, and their appreciation of what the Mission hospital had contributed to the welfare of the people of Basrah.

Dr. Bennett had a long sad convalescence and when he was able to travel he and Matthew left, also not to return.

The typhus epidemic was now under control and it was known how to cope with it. As time went on we read of similar epidemics in other war areas and the precautions taken by those who nursed typhus patients. They wore hospital gowns which completely covered them and hip boots and long gloves to protect them from the body lice which carry the disease. John and I had gone about freely in our ordinary clothes helping to nurse the patients in our stricken hospital, coming in close contact with them over a period of many days. We shuddered to think of the risks we had unknowingly taken.

In the spring of 1916 Gertrude Bell came to Iraq, and we began the cherished friendship with that remarkable character which continued as long as she lived. Miss Bell was one of the great Englishwomen who made herself a part of the Near East, and had a share of influencing history in the Arab world. Before the war she had been an intrepid traveller in the Arabian deserts, and had learned to know intimately Arab tribes and Arab personalities. This experience was of great value to the military administration, and she was formally attached to the political department upon her arrival in Basrah. Her first task was to organize all the available information about the Arab tribes, and to compile a Gazeteer. John was very knowledgable about tribal Iraqis from his extensive tours in the marshes and desert during his first term, and she constantly consulted him. Her erect figure, and her eager animated face crowned with gray hair, became familiar in our home, and her delightful human qualities, her sparkle and intelligence and zest for life, made her a most welcome companion.

One day I came in from school and found her and John kneeling in a devotional attitude in front of the window-seat in our drawing-room.

"My goodness, Gertrude," I exclaimed, "what a surprise to see you and John apparently having a word of prayer together!" Of course I had seen his maps and charts spread out in front of them.

After she had seen his first Arabic grammar, of which she thoroughly approved, Miss Bell sent him the following jingle:

"V is Van Ess, he once wrote a book,

Perhaps you have seen it, or a copy you took,

He deserves a gold medal, without any doubt,

Not for what he put in, but for what he left out."

He replied promptly:

"G is for Gertrude, of the Arabs she's Queen,

And that's why they call her *Om el Muminee*,*
If she gets to Heaven (I'm sure *I'll* be there!)
She'll ask even Allah 'What's your tribe, and where?' "

During this difficult period of the war, when Turkish resistance in the north of Iraq was strong and the British forces were meeting with reverses, Gertrude Bell was frequently sent to enlist the co-operation of the Bedouin sheikhs in the campaign against the Turks and Germans. On one such occasion, when she was received none too cordially by the sheikh of a refractory tribe, she put the British case aptly, implying the advantages to his tribe if they allied themselves with England, and ended on a note of assurance and daring. The sheikh cogitated for a few moments and then addressed his followers:

My brothers, you have heard what this woman has to say to us. She is only a woman, but y'Allah she is a mighty and a valiant one. Now, we know that God has made all women inferior to men. If the women of the Angleez are like her, the men must be like lions in strength and valor. We had better make peace with them.

Gertrude had no interest whatever in Arab women, and was curiously insensitive to the importance of the religion of Islam, in which she likewise had no interest. She and I had many heated discussions, and I often told her that knowledge of life in the harems was essential to an understanding of the character and psychology of Arab men. I also tried to impress upon her the profound influence of their religion on social and political conditions. One day in exasperation I exclaimed,

"I have sufficient regard for your intelligence, Gertrude, to think that if you knew anything about either of these subjects, you would hold different opinions."

She laughed and said, "Touché!"

In the spring of 1916, T. E. Lawrence was sent to Iraq from Egypt as a liaison officer, and at once went up the river "where the battle was raging," as Gertrude Bell said. On his return to Basrah she brought him to see us, and on May 8th I recorded in my diary that he "had a long confab with John." He was an unimpressive young man at this time, and had very little influence on the Arabs of Iraq. How little did we foresee that he was one day to become the legendary "Lawrence of Arabia."

*Mother of the Faithful

At this time we formed a lasting friendship with another person destined to become something of a legend. St. John Philby was in the Political Department in Basrah when we first knew him. We saw a great deal of him, and always found him stimulating and provocative, not to say controversial. He amazed us by frequently attending the Sunday morning service in our little mission church. He told us frankly that the reason he came was to hear John preach in Arabic! He assured us that he learned many fine points of language and grammar from the sermon. Later he served in Baghdad, and was then transferred to Jordan. Eventually he left British service and went to the Hejaz to join Ibn Saud. He became a Muslim and wrote many books which are now classics about the Arabian peninsula.

Many years later, when my son-in-law was in the American Embassy at Jidda, he and my daughter frequently met Philby.

"Your father was the master, and I was the pupil," the great man declared to her.

Our chief mainstay in the summer of 1916 was Major Bullard. He and John would discuss endlessly the events taking place on the other side of Arabia, as well as our near-by part of the war. In June of that year the Arab Revolt had begun in Mecca, when Sherif Hussein declared himself and his people against the Turks. The British and French governments called him King of the Hejaz; he styled himself King of the Arab countries. He had been negotiating with the British in a series of letters known as the McMahon correspondence (described by our friend in a book, written after he had become Sir Reader Bullard, as "a masterpiece of ambiguity"). At any rate it seemed clear that after the war, all Arab lands except Aden might hope to be independent, and that an Arab Caliphate was to be recognized. The reverberations of this decisive act in the progress of Arab nationalism were felt all over the Arab world.

For relief from war and politics, Major Bullard and I would fall back on English literature. We were both Dickens and Jane Austen devotees, and extremely fond of The Oxford Book of English Verse. On hot summer evenings we would sit on our roof and quiz each other on locating quotations from the less familiar poems, or haranguing interminably as to which ten English sonnets we would save, if all the rest must be lost. We agreed on five or six, but after that would argue heatedly in support of our favorites.

Later that summer I went to Simla for a short holiday. I

travelled to Bombay on a troop ship, a favor secured for me by
Gertrude Bell's good offices, and was plied with champagne by
kind General St. John when I was seasick in the monsoon. I had
the companionship of our civil surgeon's wife, Mrs. David
Forbes Borrie, destined to be a lifelong friend.

In Bombay I had the pleasure of shopping for Miss Bell—a
very "clothes conscious" person, as anyone knows who has read
her *Life and Letters*. She had asked me to try to get her some
thin dresses, and I told her I had seen nice ones at a specialty
shop near the Taj Mahal Hotel, but I thought they were probably very expensive. She exclaimed:

"My dear, pay whatever you have to, I *must* have clothes!"

In Simla I was the guest of Major and Mrs. Tyrell; we had
learned to know him well in Iraq early in the war, and he was
now on the General Staff in India. They were extremely good
to me, and I had the pleasure of meeting many other officers I
knew who were in "The Hills" (as the Himalayas were always
called) on leave. Sometimes it was difficult to identify them in
civilian dress, as I had only known them in uniform on active
service.

Not so pleasant was my encounter with two determined
ladies who had come out from England to investigate the faulty
medical facilities for IEFD in the disastrous campaign against
the Turks. They heard that I was staying with the Tyrells and
that I lived in Basrah, and they courteously but insistently
asked to meet me. They plied me relentlessly with the most
searching questions; unfortunately I knew a great deal about the
sorry state of affairs, for many officers whom we knew well had
been wounded up country and sent down to the base under
shocking conditions, and had told us all about it. Some, alas,
did not live to reach their destination. I had had a pitiful
reminder of this for some months, in the presence of a little
seluki puppy (a kind of greyhound) whose master had left it
with me to care for until he came back. He was one of those
who did not return.

Shortly after my return to Basrah, an event of great interest
to us took place in Kuwait. A durbar of Arab sheikhs was held
there in November, 1916. Sheikh Mobarek of Kuwait and
Sheikh Khazal of Mohammerah (now Khoramshahr) were both
already under treaty relations with the British, and with them
on this historic occasion was Ibn Saud of the Nejd—later to be
King of Saudi Arabia. All three declared their adherence to the

British cause, in the presence of Sir Percy Cox, Chief Political
Officer of the Occupied Territories and the Gulf.

After the durbar, Ibn Saud paid a visit to the Mesopotamian
area of war, where he was shown all the British military installations and the most modern means of waging war. He was greatly
impressed with what he saw, according to Gertrude Bell, who
dropped in often to see me, and kept me informed in her own
sprightly and inimitable way of what was going on. John saw
the great man, but I did not, as I was more or less in retirement
during those months. I was awaiting the arrival of my first baby,
who was born in January, 1917; a boy, to the great joy of all
our Arab friends.

When a boy is born, the father is told, "Praise the Lord, you
have a son," but if the baby is a girl the information is conveyed
by the words, "Praise the Lord, the mother is well."

My mother and sister had braved the hazards of travel under
war conditions, and had come from America by way of the
Pacific to spend the winter with us. Helen had just been graduated from Mount Holyoke College, and she was a tremendous
asset to Basrah in every way. She ran my school for me most
competently; she cooperated with Lady Cox in a canteen for
British soldiers; and she brightened the lives of many young
British officers and American YMCA men. She had a rose-
colored suit with a large rose felt hat which was the favorite,
among her many attractive outfits, of these girl-deprived young
men.

We had all the young American and Canadian YMCA
secretaries assigned to work with the British forces in this
theatre of war to a Thanksgiving supper which was quite
literally a roaring success, in spite of the scarcity of ladies. The
Cantines were back from furlough and we had a doctor tempo-
rarily replacing Dr. Bennett, but without his wife. Mother and
Mrs. Cantine, and Helen and I, were the feminine contingent. I
had made mince-meat (which is delicious using date-syrup instead of molasses, and pomegranate juice for cider) and we had
little individual mince and pumpkin pies, after the creamed
chicken and "fixings" had disappeared. We couldn't get turkey
enough for so many people. Mother had stuffed dozens of dates
and Helen made huge pans of divinity fudge. John and Mother
worked out a very successful program of stunts and games,
culminating in a hilarious debate on the subject, "Resolved, that
mince pie has done more for civilization than pumpkin pie."

In all our celebrating we were deeply conscious of the real meaning of the day. I have often felt that when we observe national holidays overseas in an alien environment, their significance is greater than it is at home. We are profoundly aware of the privilege and blessing of being Americans and we do not take it for granted.

We had a most happy family winter, and didn't feel it was heartless to enjoy ourselves, because the general atmosphere of Basrah had become much more cheerful. At last the tide of war in the Mesopotamian campaign was turning in favor of the Allies. On March 11, 1917, Baghdad was captured, and General Maude announced in a public proclamation that Britain would give Iraq control over her own affairs as soon as it was practicable. This, he pointed out, would be the first time since the Mongol conquests that Iraq would be free of foreign domination.

We left for furlough at the end of March, travelling from Basrah to Bombay in a British troop ship, the "Ellenga." It was full of Turkish prisoners, on their way to concentration camps in India, and John hobnobbed with them all the way, greatly interested in the tales they had to tell. One of them obligingly acted as babysitter for us, carrying the small John in his arms up and down the deck while we were below having our meals. Halfway down the Persian Gulf we joined a convoy of five other ships, escorted by H.M.S. "Juno" which saw us to Bombay. From there we went on to Colombo, where we met my mother and Helen. They had left Basrah ahead of us to do some visiting in India. We all then proceeded to America by way of the Far East.

All the way along we followed the war news with keenest interest, and we were very happy when the United States came into the war that spring. We had tried to maintain scrupulously our official neutrality in Basrah during the war years, difficult though it was. John had been fully convinced that the presence of the English in Iraq was the best thing for that country, then and later, and he summed up his position in a statement made in one of his published articles:

I am not British, nor do I have any British affinity, but any fair-minded man will have to admit that in Mesopotamia Britain is today showing the world that she is trying to live up to her programme of justice, magnanimity, and **civilization**.

As a neutral my husband had been very useful in communicating, through the Red Cross in Geneva, with the American Embassy in Constantinople on behalf of former Turkish subjects in the part of Mesopotamia under British occupation. These people were frantic for news of relatives and friends in Asiatic Turkey, sometimes as near as Baghdad, from whom they were completely cut off. Especially were they concerned for the men who were presumably still obliged to fight in the Turkish army. The news which John was able to obtain for them was not always good, but they were thankful to have any sort of communication established.

During our furlough year in America, we were both asked constantly to make speeches telling about the dramatic events we had seen in our area of the war. When these were to church groups, we had to make it clear that we were representing missions and were not merely reporters. The exciting happenings we had witnessed and in which we were sometimes involuntary participants were a part of our background and incidental to our lives. Missionaries were trusted and consulted because they had no political or business axe to grind, and were concerned solely with the welfare of the Arab people.

My husband was often called into consultation in Washington with the State Department, which appreciated his detached and well-informed point of view. He addressed different organizations all over the country and wrote numerous articles for publication.

We left America in the autumn of 1918, and were at sea on the Pacific when the joyful news reached us that the war was over. We heard all the war and armistice news when we reached Manila, and then continued what seemed like an incredibly slow voyage to Calcutta. We crossed India by train, and from Bombay were again able to travel by troopship up the Persian Gulf, thanks to our friends at British headquarters. How happy we were to reach Basrah shortly before Christmas.

A new chapter in history was about to begin, and we were full of anticipation as to the future of our corner of the Arab world.

X

Spy in the House

Our adventure with a spy during the first World War deserves a chapter to itself. For years I wanted to write up the story, but I couldn't decide on the sequence of events, and I didn't want to put the cart before the horse. I used to relate it at dinner parties (on request only) and found that it was effective either way.

Before World War I, the United States had a consulate at Muscat, the capital of Oman, on the Arabian Sea. The place became increasingly less important, and after the death in Muscat of the last American consul to be posted there, the office was closed. The Consulate effects were packed up in a very rough-and-ready fashion by the local staff and sent by ship up the Persian Gulf to my husband in Basrah for safe-keeping.

The war had begun then, and everything in this part of the world was in great confusion. Baghdad, where our nearest Consulate had been, was behind Turkish lines, and lower Mesopotamia was under British military occupation. We of the mission were the only Americans in the whole region.

The Muscat "effects" included office furniture, desks, files and stationery, and one very small box, strapped with iron and sealed, and labelled "Consular Jewels." This was the subject of a good many jokes, and our colleagues twitted us about the fabulous pearls and diamonds which we might be harboring. John surmised that a native clerk, who didn't know much English, probably looked up the Arabic word for "valuables" in his Arabic-English dictionary and picked the first equivalent given, which happened to be "jewels." He thought that very likely the consular seal and other such things might be in the box. Anyhow, it was all stowed securely in a locked storeroom on the ground floor of our old Arab house, and we thought no more about it.

We went to India for our summer vacation that year, to a hill station in the Himalayas, and on our return, in the autumn of 1915, came to Karachi to take ship for the Persian Gulf. While we were in Karachi my husband and I went to the American

Consulate to get instructions as to what to do with the government property in our custody.

When he heard about the little box labelled "Consular Jewels" the consul leapt from his desk.

"Good grief, Van Ess, can it be that it's the Muscat copy of
the State Department Code Book?"

He said they had been frantic trying to locate it, for of course
it should never have gone out of the keeping of an American
citizen. In time of war it was extremely serious to have a copy
lost. They had been unable to get in touch with the local staff
which had been in the Muscat Consulate, which obviously had
not informed them about what had been done with the consulate property after the death of the unfortunate consul.

So he told John to open the box as soon as we got back to
Basrah, and to cable him—I think the word was to be "mince
pie" if it was the code book, and "apple pie" if it wasn't. If it
was, we were instructed to burn it up, page by page, in the
utmost secrecy. It was, and we did, and I could never feel more
important and Secret-Service-ish in my life than I did as I sat
and poked the fire with a Turkish bayonet until the last page
was consumed in the flames.

Now for Part Two.

This goes back to the previous spring before our trip to
Karachi and our destroying the code book.

We came back from church one Sunday morning with the
Bennetts, our medical colleagues. We stopped at their house on
the hospital compound and saw on the verandah a pile of
luggage, and just inside the front door a stranger was waiting.
She introduced herself as Mrs. Johnson, and said she had just
arrived on the mail boat from Bombay. She was hoping to get
up to Baghdad to visit a sister.

"Didn't you know that there is a war going on up here," we
said, "and that Baghdad is still in the hands of the Turks?"

She replied, "I hoped the British would soon be taking
Baghdad, and that I could get through."

We inquired her sister's name and her brother-in-law's business, and he was no one that we had ever heard of. "Mrs.
Johnson" had so little accent that it was impossible to tell her
origin—she might have been a Canadian, New Zealander, South
African, or an English or American woman who had "been
around." She was of an indeterminate age as well.

The Bennetts took her into their house to stay with them, as we of the mission always did any travellers in those days. She behaved so strangely on her very first day that Dr. Bennett and my husband felt it was wise to inform the authorities that we knew nothing about her and that she had no credentials.

Wilhelmina Holzhauser, who lived with the Bennetts, had stayed at home with a cold that morning instead of going to church as usual. She was in her room on the second floor, and heard someone in the hall; she looked out of her door and saw a strange woman emerging stealthily from the Bennetts' bedroom, and eyeing the other doors in the upper hall. Obviously she assumed that none of the family were at home. That night the guest kept her light on till after two o'clock, and Wilhelmina heard her rustling papers and moving luggage and furniture around.

On Monday Mrs. Johnson approached our hospital dispenser, a Christian Arab whom she took to be a Turk because he was wearing a fez. (As a matter of fact, he was still technically a Turkish subject.) She asked him to get her a little boat so that she could go to a ship anchored in the harbor. It was a cargo ship, and the captain was allegedly a friend of people she had met in India. Before she made her trip to the ship, she asked our dispenser to buy her a complete outfit of Turkish clothes for herself—but not to let the mission folk know. Naturally, the first thing he did was to tell Dr. Bennett!

By Thursday she was behaving so suspiciously that the chief of the Military Police, Major Gregson, decided that he would search her belongings. He got Mrs. Bennett to let him and two assistants into the house and up to Mrs. Johnson's bedroom while the family was at dinner, and pressed Miss Holzhauser into service to help them go through her things.

They found black satin evening slippers, whose red heels were hollow but empty; pockets in the band of her sun helmet and her corsets which could easily have contained papers; pockets also in her bloomers and the wristbands of her blouses. A Spanish cookbook contained many written notations—names and data of prominent Arabs in Basrah and Zobeir (and how annoyed some of them were, when they were subsequently called on the carpet and asked for explanations!). Whatever she may have brought that was incriminating, she had passed on in the course of her mysterious expeditions when she first arrived, but her behavior had aroused sufficient suspicion to make the British authorities take her into custody anyway.

When she had finished her last dinner at the Bennetts and come into the livingroom, Major Gregson was waiting and informed her politely that she was to be searched and then taken to a British ship in the harbor, which was being used as a temporary detention camp. Mrs. Bennett and Miss Holzhauser took her into the study and undressed her, and as well as scrutinizing all the clothes she had been wearing, they were asked to give her a thorough physical examination. They supplied her with a fresh outfit of clothes—underwear, a pretty cream shantung dress of Christine Bennett's, a wool stole, and as Wilhelmina said sadly afterwards, "an almost new pair of brown shoes."

The next day Major Gregson reported to us with great amusement that as soon as they reached the ship Mrs. Johnson went to her cabin, and emerged a few minutes later wrapped in an army blanket. She then marched to the ship's rail and threw *all* the mission ladies' clothes overboard!

He later on talked to her by the hour, but could never get anything out of her. In an early interview she demanded from him,

"Why did you make those women search me instead of doing it yourself? I wouldn't have minded, I'm not deformed!"

And Major Gregson, who was "hard-boiled" if ever anyone was, said with a chuckle as he told us about it,

"Do you know, I was quite embarrassed!"

She used to laugh at him when he was interviewing her, and say in a teasing way,

"Don't you wish you knew who I am, and where I came from, and what people I've been in touch with?"

I have often said that I could have been a much better spy than she was. If she had settled in with the mission, professing deep interest in either hospital work or my school, and offered to help us while waiting to get to her sister, it would have disarmed any suspicions we might have had and she could have stayed on with us indefinitely. However, she probably brought documents that had to be passed on immediately. Her friend on the cargo boat got his ship quietly out of port soon after her arrival. She was ultimately sent to an internment camp in India, where she presumably stayed until the end of the war.

Months after she had been deported, Major Gregson came to see John, as he often did, and said to him:

Van Ess, we have found out that Mrs. Johnson made a mistake when she went to the Bennetts' house: she ought to have come to you. She even had a map of your house, with different places marked on it. Did you have something which she might possibly have wanted?

To which my husband replied—and he would have made a very good diplomat if he hadn't been a missionary—"Gregson, I never give information away, I only trade it. If you'll tell me the whole story of such-and-such an affair" (some British top secret which I've now forgotten) "I'll tell you what I had, though I didn't know it at the time, that Mrs. Johnson was after."

And so, in return for information received, the American missionary told the head of the British military police about the Muscat Consulate copy of the State Department Code Book, which during the days when our spy had been at large in Basrah, was practically under our feet, in a little box with the innocent and misleading label of "Consular Jewels."

XI
1918-1939 A Kingdom is Born

On one of my furloughs I was giving an informal talk to a small group of Mount Holyoke alumnae, and one of my friends asked where I had lived in the Near East.

"Well," I answered, "first I was in a province of the Ottoman Empire; then I was in an area under military occupation; after that in a mandated country; and now I live in the Kingdom of Iraq."

"Dear me," she commented sympathetically, "how hard it must have been to move so often!"

To which my rejoinder was,

"I never moved at all, I stayed right in one place."

It was indeed history that moved. For two years after we returned to Basrah (1918–1920) the country was under military occupation, and negotiations about a treaty with Turkey dragged on at Sevres. Arab nationalistic aspirations were increasing in the Arab world, and the leaders were eager to see the commitments in the McMahon-Hussein correspondence carried out.

I heard my Arab women friends in the harems discussing President Wilson's famous Fourteen Points with great enthusiasm, if without much discrimination. The twelfth point laid down the principle that the non-Turkish nationalities then under Turkish rule should be assured an absolutely unmolested opportunity of autonomous development. Wilson was a tremendous hero throughout the Near East at this time, and as Americans we had the advantage of basking in his reflected glory.

An Anglo-French Declaration in November, 1918, had contained the assurance that the aim of France and Great Britain was

the complete and final liberation of the peoples who have for so long been oppressed by the Turks, and the setting up of national governments and administrations that shall derive their authority from the free exercise of the initiative and choice of the indigenous populations.

In the meantime we were hearing from both our English and Arab friends in Baghdad of the tense situation which was developing there. London and Baghdad had been corresponding about the form of government for Iraq, and there was wide difference of opinion between the Foreign Office and the India Office, and the people on the spot.

The British attempted to get an idea of public opinion, to find out whether the Arabs of Iraq would favor a single Arab state, from Mosul to the Persian Gulf, under British tutelage; if so, should there be an Arab head, and whom would they prefer? The Kurds were against Arab government and favored British administration. The Arabs wanted Mosul included, and thought it desirable to have an Arab ruler.

Basrah Vilayet, which we knew best, was very much detached from the whole discussion. Basrah was never politically minded —one of the reasons which made it such a pleasant place to live. It was the port of the country, and faced the various Gulf sheikhdoms and India. Agriculture and trade were the chief activities. There were many tribal areas in the region. John was privately of the opinion that Southern Iraq would, ironically, have preferred the Turks, to whose ways they were accustomed, and who were co-religionists and possessed the Caliphate. Their second choice would have been the British, whose administration they had found quite acceptable during the war. They were never really interested in independence except academically, and recognized that they had no trained leadership. Wilson's Fourteen Points were wonderful ideas to talk about, but when it came down to actual facts, most people wanted merely a stable regime which would enable them to lead their own lives in peace and security. Leave politics to the politicians in Baghdad.

Gertrude Bell had moved with the Political Office to Baghdad in the spring of 1917, soon after it was captured from the Turks. We always saw her whenever she came down to Basrah, and heard her views on the state of the world. She attended the Peace Conference in Versailles in 1919, and conferred frequently with T. E. Lawrence there. Lawrence's great hero, Emir Feisal, was present, representing Arab interests on behalf of his father, King Hussein of the Hejaz. At the moment Feisal was precariously administering Syria, where he was to be king for a few months in 1920. Later, after he had been expelled from

Damascus by the French, he was to be Gertrude's great hero
too, when he eventually became king of Iraq.

The Peace Conference was also attended by Colonel A. T.
Wilson (later Sir Arnold Wilson), acting civil commissioner in
Iraq, who was called in to help Miss Bell expound to the experts
on Western Arabia the very different conditions in Iraq.

"A. T." was a great friend of John's; they saw eye to eye on
the problems of the current situation and their solutions would
have been nearly identical. John considered Colonel Wilson the
brains of Sir Percy Cox's administration; he recognized that Sir
Percy had an impressive facade and was an imposing figurehead,
but he often exclaimed in private,

"He is just a rubber stamp for Lord Curzon!"

A. T. Wilson and Gertrude Bell attempted to enlighten the
Arab experts at the Peace Conference about the Shiah Muslim
element in Iraq (of which they knew nothing), the trouble to be
anticipated from the Kurds in Mosul Vilayet, and the increasing
power and importance of Ibn Saud in the Arab world.

John heard about it all with the deepest interest direct from
"A. T." whom he went to Baghdad to visit in the summer of
1919.

I had spent the month of June at the Officers' Hospital, "Beit
Na'ama," a large and pleasant country house on the river some
miles south of Basrah, which had been taken over by the British
early in the war. I had sand-fly fever and various other complications, and the Sisters' Ward in the comfortable well-run hospital was a haven of rest. The British authorities felt, quite
rightly, that our mission hospital and all its staff had been a
casualty of war, and that the least they could do was assume the
responsibility whenever any of us in the mission needed medical
care. I was given a passage on a hospital ship to Bombay and so
was my two-year old son, and two friends who were living with
us.

These were Ruth and Rachel Jackson, now honored emeritus
missionaries, who had given a lifetime of notable service to girls'
education in our different mission stations. In 1918 they were
eager girls just out of college, daughters of one of my mother's
childhood friends with whom she had always kept up a close
intimacy. During our furlough they were visiting mother in the
Church Settlement House in Chicago of which she was then the
head, and one day at luncheon John said to them lightly,

"Why don't you girls come back to Basrah with Dorothy and me in the fall, and see the world and visit the mission?"

So here they were, just when they were needed, to look after my little boy and me on the long journey to South India. This was the only time in my life that I have travelled on a stretcher, when I was moved from the hospital to the spotless white ship with a huge Red Cross on each side; and again when we disembarked at Bombay. I was the only "wounded officer" on the hospital ship—all the other patients were Indian private soldiers, who filled the large wards—and the Australian matron nursed me herself with skill and devotion.

We spent the summer of 1919 in Kodai Kanal, a resort high in the beautiful Pulni Hills of South India, which I was to know well in future years. In October we returned joyfully to Basrah, and at the end of the year my little girl was born. She was named Alice for my mother, and no one commiserated with either John or me because the baby wasn't a boy. All our friends knew how much we wished for a daughter, and their felicitations were sincere.

One of the great events of early 1920 in Iraq was the opening of the railroad between Basrah and Baghdad in January. On the first trip, the train was full of dignitaries, and a large tea party was held in the Baghdad Railway Station upon arrival. Ruth and Rachel Jackson enjoyed the exciting experience of making one of these early train journeys to Baghdad, and had a memorable sojourn in the historic old city before they left us to return to America.

In the spring of 1920 Gertrude Bell came down to Basrah to meet her father, Sir Hugh Bell, who was travelling out by sea to visit her. He was an iron-master in northern England, a man of wealth, culture, and charm, whom it was a privilege to know. While Gertrude was awaiting the arrival of his ship, she spent long hours in our house, talking with John, and receiving all her Arab friends in John's study, where word had gone forth that she would be "sitting." She wanted to sound out feelings in the provinces as to what form the new government of Iraq should take. She was also anxious to discuss it with my husband and me, for she valued and respected our opinions even when she disagreed with them. At this time Gertrude Bell was changing her attitude, as she so often did about persons as well as ideas, on the organization of the new Arab state. In 1918 she had expressed herself strongly against an Arab emir and a "brand-new court," in favor of having Sir Percy Cox head a civil administration. But in 1919 she had been with Lawrence at the Peace Conference and had undoubtedly been influenced by his very pro-Arab stand. Now she was all for an Arab state with an Arab head, and British advisers. John held firmly to the opinion of A. T. Wilson, that Iraq was not yet ready for independence. Wilson advocated a British High Commissioner and a government of Arab ministers with British advisers. Under this regime Iraqi leadership would be trained and made ready eventually for the establishment of a self-contained Nation of Iraq. John felt strongly that the tribal loyalties should be utilized, and be built into the new state as a valuable ingredient. He and I both greatly regretted the animosity which was developing between Gertrude and "A. T." as their opinions diverged and clashed.

Wilson was generous to her in his book *Loyalties*, but her published letters and papers contain sharp and often unjust criticisms of him which are unworthy of her. She must indeed have been a thorn in his flesh while they were colleagues in the Political Office in Baghdad.

During those lovely spring days in March, Gertrude sat with her feet tucked under her in true Arab style, on a settee in John's study, smoking his cigarettes and arguing with him interminably, but always amicably.

"But Gertrude!" he would exclaim:

You are flying in the face of four milleniums of history if you try to draw a line around Iraq and call it a political entity! Assyria always looked to the west and east and north, and Babylonia to the south. They have never been an independent unit. You've got to take time to get them integrated, it must be done gradually. They have no conception of nationhood yet.

Then they would discuss the tribes, to whom Miss Bell was just as devoted as John, and she would say confidently,

"Oh, they will come around!"

The mandate for Iraq was given to Britain at the San Remo conference a month later. Events continued to move slowly, and in the summer of 1920 there was a revolt in the Euphrates area. We were in the mountains of South India for part of the time, and followed the news with absorbing interest. Years later (1942) John summarized this chapter of Iraq history thus:

The rebellion of 1920 has been cited as a heroic effort on the part of patriotic Nationalists to throw off the British yoke, and, indeed, as the determining factor which finally induced the British to yield to the program of early independence. As a matter of fact, the rebellion of 1920 began in the middle Euphrates region among tribes whom I know very well, since I lived among them off and on for seven years. They had been chronically in rebellion against the Turks and have been chronically in rebellion against the Iraq government ever since. The motivation was more that of Shiah versus Sunni than anything else, and was fostered by the religious leaders of the shrine cities who have always fished in troubled waters. No Tigris tribes, and in fact no people of Basrah, Baghdad or Mosul, took part in the rebellion at all except Jemil Medfai, and he only at a distance. There were some disturbances in the Diyala region near Baghdad, but they were in no sense part of the rebellion as such.

The rebellion was put down by a British expeditionary force which was said to cost the British Exchequer about forty million pounds sterling, and caused an estimated ten thousand total casualties on both sides.

Sir Percy Cox had been appointed high commissioner for Iraq and arrived in October, 1920, and his immediate task was to form some sort of Arab government.

At this point, our friend Sayyid Talib Pasha el Naqib came into the picture. He had returned to Iraq from Eygpt early in 1920, and was regarded by the Nationalist party in Syria as the spokesman of national aspirations. All former Turkish deputies were invited to a meeting in Baghdad by the civil high commissioner, and Talib was elected president. Their purpose was to discuss the formation of a National Assembly. He also acted as an intermediary with the insurgents in the insurrection in the summer of that year. Talib openly declared his aspirations to become emir of Iraq, and worked assiduously to attain this end. I have often speculated on what the course of history would have been had he been chosen instead of Feisal. Would the government have evolved into a more democratic form, and would the violence of the 1958 revolution have been unnecessary? Talib was a native son, but he had made many personal enemies over the years, by whom he was feared and distrusted. The British were suspicious of him, and considered his ambitions more personal than patriotic. It was a great pity that his immense prestige and his real qualities of leadership could not have been utilized in a constructive way. Perhaps his personality was more suited to mediaeval times than to helping build a modern state. At all events he was passed over, and the old Naqib of Baghdad somewhat reluctantly became president of a Council of State, to serve as an interim government. Sayyid Talib Pasha was persuaded, also reluctantly (as somewhat beneath his dignity), to be minister of interior, with Philby as his adviser.

In February, 1921, Gertrude Bell appeared on our doorstep one fine day at lunch time, and told us in great excitement that she was off to a conference in Cairo with Sir Percy Cox. They were to sail from Basrah on H.M.S. "Hardinge" before dawn, and in the meantime she was spending the day with us. She and John had a great visitation, for he was of course deeply interested in the gathering of Middle East experts summoned by Winston Churchill, in which the future of Iraq and other Arab countries was to be discussed. He tore himself away with difficulty and went back to school, and Gertrude disappeared into our nursery. When I went later to tell her that John was back and tea was ready, I found her sitting on the floor with small John and baby Alice, both deeply absorbed. She announced gleefully,

"We are making a stew of mice in John's sun-hat!"

She assured the children that she would be back after tea to go on with the game, and they unwillingly let her get up, shake down her skirts, and leave the nursery with me. Alas, while we were drinking our tea, a message came from Sir Percy Cox that the "Hardinge" was to go out on the afternoon tide, and that Miss Bell must come at once. She rushed in to bid the children goodbye and to explain why she could not carry out her promise. Young John lifted up his voice and wept, loudly and disconsolately, and though the baby was too small to understand what it was all about, she cried heartily in sympathy, and it took me till their bedtime to console them.

At the Cairo Conference it was decided that Britain should support the candidature of Emir Feisal, son of Sherif Hussein of Mecca, for the throne of Iraq.

When Sir Percy Cox and Miss Bell returned to Baghdad, they found that during their absence Sayyid Talib had been diligently campaigning for the Naqib of Baghdad. He undoubtedly counted on the fact that he himself would be next in line, and as the Naqib was old and infirm he might not have long to wait. He overreached himself, and finally settled his fate by a very indiscreet speech on a public occasion. He was arrested—regrettably, in a manner unworthy of his own eminent position and of the dignity of the British government, as he was leaving a teaparty at Lady Cox's house—and exiled to Ceylon, in April, 1921.

(He died in Munich in 1929, and was buried in Zobeir, near Basrah, with full honors. He was commemorated throughout the Arab world as one of the early leaders in the "Arab Awakening.")

"Sidi Feisal" finally reached Iraq early in the summer of 1921. His reception in Basrah was lukewarm, and the Arab governor, riding at the head of the procession, begged the bystanders,

"For Allah's sake, cheer!"

John had a long conversation with him the day of his arrival, and was not particularly impressed by him at that time, as he gave little indication of the potentialities which were to develop later. However, this was the beginning of a personal friendship between them which increased and strengthened as long as Feisal lived. John was to be his guest at the palace in Baghdad more than once, and the Arab monarch and the American missionary had long intimate discussions about the welfare of Iraq.

Feisal's reception in Baghdad was outwardly more enthusiastic than the one in Basrah, but he was conscious of cross-currents, and not at all assured of his position. The referendum of the country, energetically promoted by the British, was unanimous in favor of Feisal with the one exception of Kirkuk. Gertrude Bell wrote to us exultantly,

"Feisal will romp in on our shoulders!"

Any election in a country where only twenty per cent of the men are literate (this was the estimated figure at that time) is unconvincing, but it was easy to ignore vague unfavorable opinions.

Feisal was crowned King of Iraq on August 23, 1921, and thereupon proceeded to consolidate his position. He was fortunate to have around him a group of capable Iraqi Arabs, who had been trained in the Turkish army, but left it during the war to ally themselves with the Arab cause.

Nuri Pasha el Said was an old friend of ours from the days

when he had been a prisoner-of-war patient in our mission hospital in Basrah in 1914.

Abdul Mehsin beg el Sa'adun was our fellow townsman; he was the son of a powerful Montafiq sheikh and had large estates in the Basrah countryside. His niece was one of my pupils. I always recalled that she came to my school to be enrolled during one of the very last days of the Turkish regime, when "Holy War" crowds were parading the streets with banners and shouting their war-cries.

Ja'far Pasha el Askari had been commander in chief of Feisal's army during the war, after he had left the Turks for the Arab side. John came to know him well, after an amusing first meeting. My husband was a very tall man, and he said that Ja'far Pasha deliberately looked him up and down, from his head to his feet and back again, when they were first introduced. Not to be outdone, John surveyed the pasha's very considerable bulk from side to side, turning his head back and forth, equally deliberately. Then they both burst out laughing, and became the best of friends. Ja'far Pasha was considered the leader of the Iraqi nationalists who returned from Syria. He was prime minister in the Iraqi government which finally confirmed the treaty with Britain, and passed the Law of the Constitution through the Constituent Assembly.

Yasin Pasha el Hashmi was another prominent figure who was to be a leader in the new state, as was also Jamil Medfai.

Ali Jowdet beg el Ayoubi, whom John characterized as "a shrewd, old-school soldier but a realistic politician" became a great friend of ours. We first knew him while he was Mutaserif of Basrah Province, when his children and ours were young and used to play together. His charming wife was a pioneer in the unveiling of Muslim women, back in the days when it took courage to endure criticism from the conservative. We had the pleasure of welcoming him and his family to the United States when he became Iraq's minister in Washington. We happened to be on furlough and the State Department asked John if he would meet him on his arrival in New York. In later years he was to be several times prime minister of Iraq, and we often saw him in Baghdad.

Another fellow-townsman of ours was a leading figure in the new government, Abdul Latif Pasha el Mendil, whom Gertrude Bell described as having "the sharp fine features of the Arab of inner Arabia, possibly the most forceful personality in the country now that Talib has gone." I had a very warm spot for him in my heart because of his personal visit to congratulate me when I had produced a daughter. We knew his whole family circle as well, and had had their children in both our schools.

Several of these great Iraqi leaders were to meet with violent deaths. Ja'far Pasha was assassinated in 1936 in a military coup d'etat led by Bekr Sidki; Abdul Mehsin beg el Sa'adun commited suicide (very rare among Muslims) because of despondency over lack of unity among the Arabs; and Nuri el Said was brutally murdered in the revolution of 1958.

During these early years of the nineteen-twenties, Gertrude Bell occupied a position in Baghdad which caused her often to be referred to as "The Uncrowned Queen of Mesopotamia." There is no doubt that she had a finger in every pie; she had the ear of Sir Percy Cox and was his intermediary with tribal sheikhs and other notables, and she took naive pleasure in feeling that she was manipulating the affairs of the new nation. She was a close personal friend of King Feisal's, and advised and assisted him on his court, the furnishing of his palace, his entertaining, and his private affairs. He was a lonely man and undoubtedly appreciated her companionship and her concern, but he must often have been embarrassed by her romantic conception of his character, and the impossibly lofty ideas she attributed to him. She had the somewhat ambiguous title of "Oriental Secretary" which applied equally well to politics and archeology.

John and I maintained a warm personal friendship with Gertrude, never affected by our frequent differences of opinion on policies and personalities in the Near East. She had no use for women in general, and was both unjust and unkind to many of them who crossed her path—a fact which I deeply deplored. But my relationship to her was perfect, and her devotion to John and me and our children is one of my richest memories of that period of our lives.

For several years we went up to Baghdad during our spring vacation, and saw a great deal of her, no matter how busy she was. She had a unique and delightful little Arab house set in a lovely garden, and she entertained beautifully.

On one of these visits it was arranged for me and Rose Tainsh, the wife of the director of railways, to go to the palace and be presented to the Queen of Iraq, whom King Feisal had recently brought over from Mecca. We found her a shy, quiet little woman, obviously ill-at-ease in the unfamiliar atmosphere of a newly established court.

Sir Percy Cox retired in the spring of 1923, with many farewell ceremonies in both Baghdad and Basrah, where full tribute was paid to his long years of distinguished service in the Gulf and Iraq. At the final garden party in Basrah, given by Arab dignitaries, he was presented with a silver date tree bearing golden fruit, and he asked John to translate his speech of acceptance and farewell into Arabic.

There followed a difficult period for Iraq, with friction between British and Iraqi nationalists, in spite of the fact that a treaty with Britain was approved by the Iraqi Parliament in June, 1924. Authority seemed divided, and there were animosities within the country. Kurds were against Arabs, tribesmen against townsmen, Sunnis against Shiahs, north against south, and progressives against reactionaries.

A cause of resentment against the British was the contrast between the very high salaries paid to British advisers and the much lower ones of Arab officials. Special privileges served to emphasize this distinction. I have never forgotten a glaring example which I once witnessed. I was travelling back to Basrah with my children after a summer in a hill station in India, and on the same ship was the wife of a deputy director of Iraq Railways, with two small children and an English nurse. As we were sailing up the river approaching Basrah, I enquired pleasantly of her if she expected her husband to be down from Baghdad to meet her.

"Indeed he will!" she exclaimed emphatically. "And he will have a special train for us to travel up. He wouldn't *dream* of letting us go on an ordinary train!"

Sure enough, when we approached the dock, we saw a puffing engine and two private railway coaches drawn up at the end of the branch line to the wharves, some miles away from the passenger station. I have often wondered what this piece of snobbery cost, both in money and goodwill.

Early in this decade, the Nairn brothers, New Zealanders, began the first regular cross-desert motor service from Baghdad to Damascus. This established communications between countries that had been widely separated for lack of travel facilities other than camel caravans, and drew the whole area of the Near East together. When we went across the desert in the spring of

1925, on our way to America on furlough, we were in an open touring car. Rutba Fort was not yet built, and our only stops were in the open desert. At midnight the whole convoy (about twenty cars, as I recall) came to a halt, a huge bonfire was built and a welcome meal of sausages, eggs, and hot tea was prepared. Our children, aged eight and five, had been sleeping like kittens, curled up on the back seat; they awoke refreshed and hopped out, delighted with this very unusual picnic.

I have always regretted that we happened to be absent from Iraq for that particular year, because in the summer of 1926, when we were in northern Michigan, we heard with sorrow of the death of Gertrude Bell in Baghdad. She had been lonely, and sad at feeling she was no longer necessary in councils of state, especially after Sir Percy Cox had gone. The king and government were becoming firmly established, but she was often profoundly disillusioned when she felt that Feisal and his ministers were falling short of her ideals for them. She was always a romantic and never a realist. Her work as Oriental Secretary during her last few years lived after her in the Museum of Antiquities in Baghdad which bore witness to her gifts as an archeologist and a historian. Unlike Lady Hester Stanhope, to whom she has often been compared, Gertrude Bell never became an eccentric, nor sacrificed the personal dignity and integrity which characterized her to the end of her life. Beside the Bedouin's campfire, or in the king's palace in Baghdad, she remained what she was—a distinguished English gentlewoman.

Another old friend of ours went into eclipse during this decade. Sheikh Khazal of Mohammerah, whose sons had been in our school, had enjoyed treaty rights with the British, and since 1909 with the oil companies. For years he had nominally owed allegiance to the Persian government, but had for all practical purposes been independent. However, when Riza Khan became Minister of War, the power of the Teheran government began to extend to the provinces, Sheikh Khazal was unwise enough to defy the central government of Riza Khan in 1924, and a force marched south against him. The revolt collapsed, and Khazal was sent to Teheran, where he died a few years later, after Riza Khan had become Riza Shah. He was well treated, but his sheikhdom ceased to exist, and his wives and descendants were scattered through Persia, Iraq, and Kuwait.

We returned to Iraq in the autumn of 1926, and found that the nation was becoming an entity, and really progressing along the lines of self-government. Land survey was carried out, public works undertaken, the system of taxation was revised, and government departments were being staffed with reasonably trained and qualified men. Much of this was due to King Feisal, who had developed real statesmanship as he advanced in his difficult task as the head of a new nation. He drew Iraqi leaders together and eased the pressure between them and their British advisers.

In 1929 our mission experienced another tragic loss. Henry Bilkert, a young clergyman, was shot and killed in a tribal raid on the desert between Basrah and Kuwait. He was accompanying Charles R. Crane, a well-known American millionaire and philanthropist, who had been one of President Wilson's commissioners to the Near East in 1919. He and Dr. Henry King of Oberlin College conducted an inquiry as to the preferences of "Greater Syria" for their future government and issued the famous King-Crane report. Now he was turning his attention to other Arab countries and was eventually to help King Ibn Saud of Saudi Arabia prospect for oil. The skirmish in which Henry Bilkert was killed was between a tribe from central Arabia, the Ajman, and a tribe near the Iraq border with whom they were disputing grazing rights and boundaries. The frontier post in Iraq did not give warning that the road was unsafe for travellers, and a bullet meant for an Iraqi Bedu struck the car in which the Crane party and Mr. Bilkert were passengers.

Our American consul in Baghdad was prepared to hold the Iraq government responsible, and to place a formal charge and ask for indemnity. My husband, as spokesman for the mission, persuaded him not to do so. Neither Mrs. Bilkert nor the mission had any desire for vengeance, nor for what would seem like blood money. To raise the issue would have caused bad feelings between the Iraqi and American governments, and injured the goodwill which the mission had won for itself over the years, and belied the principles on which it was founded. This attitude, which became publicly known, made a deep impression on the Arabs of Iraq and Kuwait, as well as the tribes.

The Basrah Airport, which was opened in 1931, had its origins in an interesting way. In the summer of 1930, my husband was preaching in St. Peter's Church, Basrah, the Anglican Church under the Bishopric of Jerusalem. It served as community church for all the English speaking residents of Basrah, and the clergymen of our mission often took charge of the services when there was no chaplain. That evening John shocked the congregation by saying, in the course of his sermon on "Dynamic Discipleship," that within a short distance of the church there were people almost dying of starvation. After the service a good friend of John's came up to him and said,

"I want to be a 'dynamic disciple'—what can I do about this?"

This was Colonel Ward (later Sir John Ward), the Director of the Port of Basrah, a church warden and a staunch supporter of the church.

The result was that he decided to reclaim a large tract of land north of the new port headquarters on the river, and build a housing project for a future labor corps made up of these very poor people. He asked my husband to round them up, and senior boys of the School of High Hope were assigned to the task. They ran into difficulties with labor contractors—"coolie tindalls" as they were called—who traditionally controlled what was a very lucrative monopoly, and resented any encroachment. However, the boys were undaunted and went directly into villages and slums, and eventually recruited a goodsized labor force. Families were housed in the new settlement, and maintained by the Port Directorate until the men were fit for work. Intended at first for storage of grain, the large open space on the river was never used for that, but became the Basrah Airport. For years it was one of the largest and most important airports in the Near East. In 1931 it was opened by King Feisal the First in a very impressive ceremony. As there were many guests present who did not know Arabic, the king called for his friend John Van Ess to come and translate his speech into English—a mark of trust and regard which touched my husband deeply.

By this time, the two were fast friends, and John wholeheartedly admired the strength and intelligence by which Feisal had welded the country together. He wrote of him:

It was Feisal who by his personal charm and infinite patience curbed the impatience of the hot-heads, schooled the tribesmen in the ways of co-operation, encouraged the fainthearted, cajoled the religious leaders, and convinced the British that Iraq was ready for independence and membership in the League of Nations in 1932.

When the ceremony took place in Geneva, at which Iraq was admitted to the League of Nations, our children were attending the École Internationale in that city. Sir Francis Humphreys, the last British high commissioner in Iraq under the Mandate, secured a ticket for our son John to attend the session. As he was going in, he met some of the Iraqi deputies who knew his father. They exclaimed:

"Come along with us, you belong with the Iraq delegation!"

So the fair-haired American school boy sat among his Arab friends on this historic occasion.

Our last meeting with King Feisal, the year before he died, was at a reception in Basrah. This was the occasion when he said to John,

"You are one of the few who have come to this land to give and not to get. By the milk of your mother, swear to me that you will always tell the Arabs the truth about themselves."

This conversation became well known to Iraqis and was widely quoted afterwards. At this same party, King Feisal sent for me, and told me how much he appreciated what I had done for the girls and women of Iraq throughout the years.

His death in 1933 was a great loss to the country. His son Ghazi who succeeded him was personally very popular, but he was young and inexperienced, and an extreme nationalist and militarist. He was killed in a motor accident in 1939 and was succeeded by his son, a very small child, as Feisal the Second, under the regency of his maternal uncle, Prince Abdul Ilah.

XII
Private Lives

Against the rich background of the Arab world, and our own work which was absorbing and satisfying, we led our private lives.

For our first five and a half years there were just our two selves, and we were fully and happily occupied in establishing our schools. We had most congenial colleagues, the Cantines, the Bennetts and Miss Holzhauser, and a very pleasant station life. Every year the annual meeting of our mission brought us all together with all our fellow missionaries, either in Basrah, or somewhere "down the Gulf." The bond between members of a mission is a very close and special one; there are times when it almost transcends the ties of blood. It is one of the most rewarding features of our life.

Our first home in Basrah was an old Arab house on the creek, built around a courtyard, and we lived in that or the one next to it (to which we moved when our first house began to fall down) for ten years. The courtyards were full of hollyhocks, and our flocks of pigeons—some of them "tumblers"—used to come and get crumbs from our breakfast, which we had on the verandah in hot weather. There is a charm and atmosphere to these old-fashioned houses which more than compensates for their inconveniences, and I have always been glad that I had the experience of living there before moving to a bungalow on the mission compound, which was our permanent home.

Our domestic servants were a motley collection. For many years we had a Goanese cook, as did most European families—a cross little man but a marvelous culinary artist. When I engaged him, I asked him if he drank (a failing very common among his compatriots) and he said indignantly,

"No Ma'am, never! I totaller!"

In the summer of 1912 John and I went to Amarah, up the Tigris River, for six weeks, and we took our staff with us. We had a ramshackle old house in bad repair, and the room next to the kitchen where our "Jao Pedro Mendez" slept was infested with scorpions. He complained to John,

"Sahib, these crabs, they pick you!"

However neither he nor we ever suffered any harm from them. His English was very limited and I had to learn to express my wishes chiefly in participles. I also had to distinguish the shades of meaning between "few few" and "plenty few," few plenty" and "plenty plenty," as well as "few cheap" and "plenty cheap," and "few dear" and "plenty dear." One *chef d'oeuvre* of his was caramel basket pudding, filled with fruit and cream, and a large handle adorned with three caramel cocks, one each for John Jr., Alice, and the short-termer. We always had this on Easter, when the contents were *blancmange* eggs tinted in different colors.

Our first butler and houseboy was an Afghan who had been John's servant in his bachelor days. Akbar was intelligent and capable, and had been an excellent servant for a group of young single men. However, he was much better suited to their somewhat erratic ways than he was to the strictly supervised regime of a Mem Sahib, and when he fell ill and was ordered a prolonged period of rest, we parted company with goodwill on both sides. When he was well, we helped him set up as a small shopkeeper, and his initiative and independence had full scope.

Our next factotum was Ali, an Arab whom we inherited from the Bennetts, and who was the prop of my existence for nearly twenty-five years. His proprietory attitude toward us and all our possessions was sometimes trying, often amusing, and always invaluable, as he looked after our interests much more thoroughly than we did ourselves. He was a real character, and the whole mission rang with "Ali stories" for years.

When we went to Baghdad *en famille* the first time, when the children were small, we went on the evening train. I said to Ali as we left the house,

"Strip the beds and put the bedding in the bathroom hamper, and I will send it and the other soiled clothes to the dhobi when I come back."

On our return, I found clean clothes and household linen spread out on our beds, and the strangest looking laundry list I had ever seen. I took it to John, as I couldn't make head or tail of it. He examined it and burst out laughing.

"It is Arabic written in Hebrew characters," he said. "Where on earth did it come from?"

"The dhobi came," he said, "and it was much better to send the wash then, than to leave dirty laundry until you came back. I couldn't let it go without having it counted, so I went out on the road and asked a Jew (begging your pardon) who was passing to come in and make a list for me, since as you know, I can't read or write myself."

"Was he willing?" I asked incredulously.

"No," answered Ali with the utmost simplicity, "but I made him do it."

Ali used to rule John with a rod of iron when the children and I were away. My husband was in the habit of taking a book or a magazine to the table for these solitary meals, and often would forget to eat. One day Ali came up and gently but firmly took the book out of John's hand.

"There is a time for everything!" he declared. "This is the time for you to eat, Sahib, not read."

I used a lovely carved Kashmir table of Mrs. Cantine's while she was on furlough, as she preferred not to put it in storage and knew that Ali and I would take good care of it. When she came back from America, I told Ali to have one of our boatmen take it down the road to her house.

"Oh no, I can't do that!" he exclaimed. "What would we have tea on?"

He loved having guests, and considered those of the mission as much his as ours. One day I came in from school and saw an extra place laid on the luncheon table.

"Who is this for, Ali?" I inquired.

"Mr. Dystra has come down from Amarah," was his reply, "and of course I invited him to stay with us. His bag is in the guestroom. He has gone to Gray and Mackenzie's but he will be back in time for lunch."

He knew every item of our belongings better than we did, and was especially vigilant in keeping track of all my silver. Every few months he scolded me because one spoon was missing from a set that had belonged to my grandmother.

"There are only eleven of this kind!" he would grumble.

"But, Ali!" I would repeat patiently. "I told you that one was lost when my mother was a little girl, she told me so."

He much preferred to blame its loss on one of the helpers whom I used to get in when we had an influx of guests, or at an annual meeting time, which he bitterly resented.

I brought a good supply of Pyrex glass percolator tops from America, and occasionally gave one to some friend in need.

When they were finished, and we needed another for our own coffeepot, Ali said to me sternly,

"If you hadn't given so many away, we would have had enough for ourselves."

When his No. 2 wife was expecting a baby (she was a niece of number 1, who had chosen her and arranged the marriage), Ali went to fetch the mid-wife in the middle of the night. He knocked loudly at her door and a call came from an upstairs window,

"Who is it?"

"Ali," was the reply.

"What Ali?" (It is a very common name.)

"Ali Van Ess!" he shouted.

He was indeed like a member of the family, and I mourned him as one when he died.

All our friends rejoiced with us when our son, John Van Ess, Jr., was born on January 14, 1917, and then when our daughter Alice came to us on December 26, 1919. My Arab women friends said,

"Now you have both bread and cheese," but I could never find out which was which.

My mother paid us two long visits, the first with my sister Helen, the year John Jr. was born, and the second when he was seven and Alice four. The only Arabic mother learned was "hot water" and "bring tea." When my Arab women friends came to see her, she found it very frustrating not to be able to understand the conversation.

"What is she saying?" mother would ask me, and when I translated she would say in a dissatisfied tone,

"It doesn't sound a bit like that!"

To my great disappointment she did not like Arab food. When we were invited out to a delectable meal, which I enjoyed so much, it was a real penance for her. I was especially fond of mahallaby, a milk pudding delicately flavored with rosewater and cardamom, and she said to me,

"I don't see how you can eat that library paste!"

She loved the desert, and greatly enjoyed the biblical atmosphere of much of our environment.

Our English and American friends all envied us because we

had "a real Grandma" in our home, and her sojourns with us brought happiness to many people besides our own family.

Basrah provided a happy setting for John Jr. and Alice. They loved the bellum picnics which were one of our favorite diversions, especially in the spring when the tides were high. We would go down our own creek to the river, and then up one of the other creeks, often overhung with blossoming oleander bushes, and find a sheltered spot. The time of the date harvest in the fall afforded them the fascinating sight of camels coming into our compound to be loaded with baskets of dates. These had been packed by our own gardeners who went up the palm trees like monkeys, supported by a kind of belt around their waists and the tree trunk, which they hitched up as they climbed.

By the time John was eleven years old, he and Alice had a little tin canoe painted green, the kind used by Arab boys, and they were allowed to go out alone—up the creek, never down. They both became expert paddlers and they used to take a picnic with them, and explore all the lesser creeks which led off the main one, far into the date gardens. They both knew how to swim, but they never had an accident with their little boat, and they had great fun on these expeditions. They spoke Arabic as freely as they did English, so they could chat with the gardeners they met in the date orchards, and the people in little farming villages.

Sleeping on the roof in summer was great fun for the children, especially as it involved a certain relaxation in discipline. Alice remarked to someone,

"I like to have Daddy be the one to see me in bed on the roof, because when Mother says she's going, she goes."

When I taxed John once for being too lenient with one of the children, he observed,

"Why do you think the Bible says 'Like as a *father* pitieth his children'?"

Both our children began their schooling with me. I used the Calvert kindergarten course for John Jr. with great success. This famous educational program by correspondence is used by American mothers all over the world. After this, it was more practical to follow the program of the Kodai Kanal school in South India, except when we were in America on furlough. For the first four grades, I taught each child from January to June, when we went to Kodai for our vacation, and they attended school. After this they went in January as boarders and had the whole school year in Kodai. This is a beautiful spot high in the Pulni Hills, southwest of Madras. There is a picturesque lake with boating for everyone, streams with waterfalls, and thick groves ideal for picnics. Fairy Falls, Bear Shola, Pillar Rocks, Coaker's Walk carved out of a steep mountainside with a superb view of the plains far below, and Mt. Perumal, were all favorite places.

The school, from small beginnings, had now grown to a good-sized institution including English-speaking children of many different organizations besides the various missions. The long vacation was from October until January, when the weather was pleasant in most of the places—Indian and father East, and the Persian Gulf and Iraq—where parents lived and worked. A teacher from the school would escort all our mission children, in the days before air travel, on the long train journey to Bombay and the ship voyage from there. At Muscat, Bahrain, Kuwait, and finally Basrah, the children would be handed over to their rejoicing parents. The teachers enjoyed these opportunities for travel, and always had a chance to go to Baghdad if they liked, and to see Ur of the Chaldees and Babylon on the way.

Kodai school at this time had only two years of high school, so when John Jr. finished these, we had to send our children elsewhere. We chose the École Internationale in Geneva, as it was co-educational and we wanted him and Alice to stay together. We knew that they would learn excellent French, and that John could prepare there for college, and take his College Board examinations. I spent the summers with them in Switzerland or France, and their father was with us the second year. We had a wonderful time exploring the lovely Swiss countryside, and staying in quiet places in the Ormont Valley and the Bernese Oberland, climbing mountains and taking walking trips. During the Christmas and Easter holidays the school arranged delightful trips for them. One winter they went skiing near the Jungfraujoch.

John went to Princeton University, where he graduated in 1938. Alice did her high school course in America; one of the years was our furlough, which we spent in Princeton, so we were all together. She went to Mount Holyoke College, as I had done, having prepared at Northfield Seminary, and was graduated in 1941.

We found many friendships over the years. Dr. David Borrie was "consular doctor," attached to the British Consulate, before World War I, and was one of our earliest and dearest friends. During the war he was a commissioned British officer and served in Iraq; then he returned to his civil status and was the founder of the excellent municipal health service in Basrah, and built a fine hospital. After our mission hospital ceased to be, he looked after us all until his untimely death in 1933. I have visited his wife, May Borrie, many times in her home in Cornwall.

"Haji" Bullard, as he became known to his family and friends when he was posted to Jidda, advanced high in the British diplomatic service, as John had predicted when we first knew him in 1914. He ended his active career as Sir Reader Bullard in Teheran, first as minister and then ambassador, and was host to the Teheran Conference in 1943, when Roosevelt, Churchill, and Stalin met there.

Sir Percy and Lady Cox, Sir Arnold Wilson, St. John Philby, and Gertrude Bell were all friends from the war years. So was Sir Henry Dobbs, who succeeded Cox as high commissioner of Iraq. We knew him first when he was our next-door neighbor in Basrah, while he was revenue commissioner. John considered him one of the most capable Englishmen who came to Iraq. He was a quick-tempered man, and there was a story current, perhaps apocryphal but certainly characteristic: he was angry about something, and walked fuming back and forth on the terrace in front of the Residency in Baghdad, finally kicking some flowerpots vigorously into the river. His wife came out and said soothingly,

"That's right, Henry—what is the use of being high commissioner if you can't kick flowerpots into the river?"

Edwin Drower (later Sir Edwin Drower) was judicial adviser to the Iraq government, and his wife Stefana was a brilliant Oriental scholar. She mastered Arabic and translated *Folk Tales of Iraq*, a delightful volume, and then turned her attention to the small and little-known sect of Mandaeans (or Sabeans) and has become the world authority on their language and religion. Ted Drower was immensely helpful to the mission in working out a legal scheme for a property-holding committee. Hitherto all mission property had to be registered in the name of an individual, which was unsatisfactory and unbusinesslike, and could have led to endless technical difficulties in case of death or disability of the legal owner.

Colonel J. C. Ward (later Sir John Ward) and his wife came to Basrah soon after the war and became our close friends. He was the founder of the Port of Basrah, and later was director of all transportation in Iraq, which included the whole railway system, and eventually the airports. He liked to talk over his problems with John and get his advice. As the years went by, large receptions and cocktail parties including both foreigners and Iraqis were very frequent, and Tilly Ward and I used to be chagrined at the way John and her "Jimmy" would always gravitate to a corner at a party, and become absorbed in conversation together to the exclusion of everyone else. However, we felt better about it when one of our Iraqi friends said appreciatively,

"We always like to see Colonel Ward and Mr. Van Ess talking confidentially together; we know it will bring about something for the good of Iraq."

Jimmy Ward had one of the first private planes in Iraq, a little two-seated Puss Moth which had belonged to the Prince of Wales. He often took John up with him, and they flew gaily all over the country together. In the late 1930s, when our son John was back in Basrah as the short-termer in the boys' school, someone said to him,

"Van Ess, no one can understand why you and your mother let your father fly with Colonel Ward. He is a very reckless pilot. Your father is too valuable a person to take such risks."

John Jr. replied drily,

"You don't know my father very well, if you talk about Mother and me 'letting' him do anything he wants to do."

I had my very first plane ride with Jimmy in the little Puss Moth, and how thrilled I was to see the river and the creeks from the air, and the head of the Persian Gulf.

Another couple whose friendship we valued greatly were "Jeff" Dowson and his wife Joy. He was an Englishman, an agricultural expert attached to the American firm of Hills Brothers, famous for Dromedary dates. He was in charge of their large experimental date plantation south of Basrah. Both Dowsons took the deepest interest in the Arabs; they learned

Arabic and built themselves into the life of the countryside where they lived. Joy worked out a program of Girl Guides adapted to illiterate Arab girls, and helped me and my colleague Christine Gosselink to incorporate it in one of our clubs for unprivileged girls, where it proved to be very successful.

Lionel Smith, adviser to the Department of Education, was another congenial associate of this period who has been our lifelong friend. He was the son of the famous A. L. Smith, Master of Balliol College at Oxford, and his sister married "Haji" Bullard. When he left Iraq, after a period of outstanding service, he became Rector of Edinburgh Academy. He was offered several other posts after accepting this one, and when I next saw him, in Scotland, I said to him,

"Lionel, we heard that you were offered the headmastership of both Eton and Harrow."

"Oh, no," he exclaimed. "Only Harrow!"

Colonel H. R. P. Dickson was a political officer in Iraq when we first knew him, but after that he served long years in Kuwait, and he and his wife became completely identified with that city. They were there from the time when it was a small Arab walled town, between the desert and the sea, till it became one of the world's leading oil capitals. I used to go down every winter to visit Dr. and Mrs. Mylrea of our mission in those early days. I tried to time it so that I would be there when the desert was carpeted with tiny blue iris, and we would go to the Dicksons' Bedouin camp. They maintained a complete encampment far out in the desert, where they often stayed for days at a time, and we had some wonderful trips with them. No foreigners knew the life of the Arabs as they did, and Dickson's books, *The Arab of the Desert* and *Kuwait and her Neighbors*, are perfect encyclopedias. I was always glad when my Kuwait visit coincided with the preparations for Muslim pilgrims to go to Mecca for the *Eed el Adh-ha*, the Feast of the Sacrifice. Camel caravans were made ready, litters for the women to ride in, in seclusion, and the gayest of harness, saddles, and saddle-bags.

John went to Baghdad very frequently; to conferences, on consultation, or to give lectures to various organizations. He learned to know all the British high commissioners in turn, and the Air Vice Marshals of the Royal Air Force, who had a large base in the vicinity of Baghdad. Each year he was asked to lecture there, and his condition was that he should be transported both ways by plane. In the early days he was strapped into a sort of camp chair next to the pilot, and before embarking had to sign what was known as a "blood chit." This freed the RAF of all responsibility if anything happened to him.

A good neighbor of ours was Captain John Morris, a bluff and hearty British engineer, who was in charge of the municipal plants for electricity and water. He lived next to us on Ashar Creek for some years, and one of the outstanding favors he did us was to "turn a mud-heap into a blessing," as he expressed it.

Our creeks were tidal, and a good deal of silt came up them, so that they needed to be dug out about once in a generation. In the early 1930's we were informed that our creek was about to be dredged. For weeks, great mounds of rich black mud were ploughed up from the creek bed by the dredging machine and flung up on the edge of our front gardens. Our lovely row of oleander bushes was buried, a long bed of beautiful cannas completely covered, rose bushes and even grape arbors were plastered with mud. Only the willows, Persian lilac trees, and of course the lordly date palms, held their heads above the enveloping flood. When the work was accomplished, the mountain range of mud in front of our houses was so high we couldn't see over it. We asked the authorities what they proposed to do about it. They replied blithely that the dredging was the responsibility of the government, but that clearing up afterwards was the affair of the individual property owners. The members of the mission were in despair. We had no funds to employ labor to carry the mud away—it would have cost a fortune for coolies—and where could it be dumped?

We were all feeling very low about the situation, when our next-door neighbor came to call. John Morris's bungalow, like our mission houses, faced the creek, but it was lower than ours and nearer to the water, and he was all but submerged under his mudbank.

"Look here," he said, "could I have my mud dumped on to the corner of your school compound?"

This was at the far end of our property, about an eighth of a mile inland from the creek. It was a low and swampy area and the mission had never been able to afford to have it filled in.

"That would be wonderful," we replied to our British friend, "but how in the world would you get it there?"

"Very simple," was his answer. "There's a light railway, with open trucks, stowed away in the port area. It is left over from the war. I'll have that brought down, run the rails from my place to your swampy corner, and my workmen can clear it away in a few days."

Then he added, incidentally,

"Wouldn't you like your mud-heap carried away at the same time? It would be very easy to shift the rails to your creek front, after they have cleared mine."

Our friend believed in direct action. Next day our school boys, and small children in the mission families, were enthralled by the fascinating sight of a miniature railway being neatly laid from the edge of the creek straight through to the far side of the school campus. Truck after truck was filled with the rich black soil; the little engine puffed its way to the swampy corner and deposited it there. Deftly the workmen took up the tracks and re-laid them in front of the mission houses, and our mountain range disappeared in its turn. The low ground was filled up, levelled off, and after a season or two when it had settled, made an extra playing field for the boys of the school and for the whole neighborhood.

An unsightly and useless part of our property became an asset, and as John Morris aptly said, a mud heap became a blessing.

Many archeologists came our way: Breasted of the University of Chicago, Clay of Yale, the Italian Chiara, and others, more than I can remember. While Sir Leonard Woolley was excavating at Ur of the Chaldees we frequently saw him in Basrah, and we had the great privilege of visiting Ur once with our children while the "dig" was in process. He gave us a personally conducted tour of the excavations, and showed us some of the treasures that had been found. They were just putting together a gaming-board (gold and ivory, as I remember) and he explained the process of reconstructing their finds. We saw the different layers of the excavated area, going back from the present time to 3500 B.C. They were just uncovering some dwelling houses, with little entryways leading to a courtyard, very similar to ones I visited in Basrah. Professor Woolley said casually, as we were looking into a doorway,

"This might be the very house that Abraham lived in."

On the last page of our guest book, in which I have the names of many visitors during the passing years, are the signatures of Sir Charles Darwin (a grandson of the great Darwin) and Agatha Christie (not on the same day—that would have been too much glory)! When Max Mallowan and his wife were to come to tea with us one afternoon, John said to me sternly,

"Now remember, it is Professor and Mrs. Mallowan who are coming here today; he is a distinguished archeologist and she is his wife, and only incidentally Agatha Christie. Don't say a word to her about her books; she is probably bored to death when people talk to her about them."

My husband deplored my fondness for thrillers, in spite of the fact that prime ministers, American presidents, and Anglican bishops, as well as hundreds of lesser folk shared my taste.

I obeyed him meekly, and we had a most pleasant afternoon with our famous guests. But as they were leaving, I couldn't resist saying to Agatha Christie Mallowan,

"I must tell you before you leave my house, that my daughter and I are two of your most faithful fans, and that your books have given us a great deal of pleasure."

An American traveller whose visit I have always remembered was a professor of English at a university somewhere in China. Our visitor had come by sea all the way, and had just arrived on the mailship from Bombay. I recall the other guests at lunch that day, because we represented such a variety of interests. One was Mrs. Robert Blackford, whose husband was an official in one of the oil companies—that tremendous industry that was about to transform the whole of the Near East; another was Stefana Drower, already recognized as an Orientalist of distinction, who was on her way back to Baghdad after an excursion up the Karun River to gather more material about Mandaean ritual from some of their priests. John was an authority on the Arabic language and Islam.

Early in the meal, our guest turned over his bread-and-butter plate to see the name of the English makers and the location of the pottery. As he did so, he apologized to me, remarking,

"This is really a compliment to your dinner-set, Mrs. Van Ess, because I am curious only about good china."

He went on to explain that when he first went to China, he became interested in Chinese porcelain, and had made such a thorough study of it that he had become an authority. He told us, what none of us who lived there had ever known, that a thousand years ago Basrah was one of the great shipping centers for China from the Far East. This was his reason for travelling to Europe by way of Iraq. From Baghdad he intended to make a detour up through Persia, to investigate the cities that had been on the caravan routes that brought goods from China by the overland route in those same far-off days.

After lunch we got him a taxi, and a high school boy who knew English, and he set off across the desert towards Zobeir about eight miles away. This had been the old port of Basrah, when the sea had come up this far, and it was marked by a ruined minaret erroneously known as Sinbad's tower, of Arabian Nights fame.

At tea-time our friend returned with a large bazaar basket filled with pieces of broken crockery.

"Every fleet of sailing boats carrying china was bound to have some accidents," he explained to us. "You can always count on finding fragments of broken jars in any harbor which was a distributing center. I was fortunate here, in finding what I was looking for near the surface, on what is now dry land."

He showed us a large curved fragment, and said,

"This is from the upper part of what you would call an Ali Baba jar. I recognize the paste, because I was the person who discovered the medieval kiln where these were produced in interior China."

He added, "It was a great good luck that I found this almost at once, I might have had a long hunt and a lot of digging."

We, who were almost speechless at the spectacular result of his expedition, exclaimed,

"But how wonderful for you to find this!"

With an almost pitying smile the professor replied,

"I knew I should find it. That is why I came to Basrah!"

In the years before air travel became common, I was always prepared for unexpected guests on Thursday, the day that the "fast mail" ship came in from India. I ordered a lunch that could be stretched indefinitely, and always had a fresh layer cake and a new batch of date cookies for tea. Government folk, missionaries, journalists, business men, archeologists, friends or friends of friends, we welcomed all comers, and we certainly "lived in a house by the side of the road."

One day I came in late for tea and heard strange voices in the living room, and as I was unusually tired, my heart sank slightly. I tidied myself and went in, and was completely disarmed by having a lady say to me,

"Mrs. Van Ess, I have been enjoying the charming New England atmosphere of your home!"

I had my grandfather's Duxbury desk and the chair that went with it, and a picture map of Massachusetts on the opposite wall. My grandmother's silver tea service was on the tea-table.

The Rev. & Mrs. John Van Ess at home in Basrah, c. 1930.

One afternoon of many that I recall vividly was when John had a group of Iraqi men in his study, and I had the dining room full of Arab ladies who had beaten a hasty retreat from the living room when several English and American couples arrived for tea. I had to escort two of the Muslim ladies by a roundabout route to my bedroom, as a young mother needed to feed her baby, and the grandmother wanted to say her prayers.

The Arabs have a saying, "The ornament of a house is the guests who frequent it," and it was indeed a pleasure and a privilege to have so many kinds of people in our home, for short or longer periods. It was, also, a wonderful experience for our children.

We were equally fortunate in our opportunities for travel. I never tired of voyages on the British India ships (unless the sea was rough) to different Gulf ports or all the way to India. The ships were comfortable and the life aboard was informal and pleasant. The deck passengers were always a fascinating spectacle to watch, and the busy seaports where the ship called, on both the Arabian and Persian sides, were of never-ending interest and entertainment. On one of our journeys, an English member of the firm of Gray and Mackenzie, the B.I. agents, was escorting a pair of huge fierce-looking bulldogs. Their names were Ida and Tiger, and the second officer took them around with him when he went to collect tickets from the deck passengers. Often these simple folk objected to parting with the mysterious pieces of paper for which they had paid good money, but the sight of Ida and Tiger straining at their leashes and baring their teeth was a great incentive to handing over their tickets without delay.

In the years before we had children, John and I took our vacations (at that time, every other year) in the Himalayas in North India, at Simla or Mussoorie. We always visited friends on the plains, and we saw Delhi, Benares, the incomparable Taj Mahal at Agra, and many other places. For some years we went to Kodai Kanal in the summer, and from there we went to Madura, Madras and Vellore. We even had a trip all the way down the west coast as far as Cape Comorin. I'll never forget one rest house where we spent a night. I was strolling around before breakfast, and asked an Indian about a very high fence all around the compound.

"Oh," he said nonchalantly, "that is to keep out the wild elephants."

One year we accepted the invitation of our missionary friends in Persia (this was before it was called Iran) and spent the summer in Hamadan, which is high in the mountains and has a delightful summer climate. Our hosts, Dr. and Mrs. Arthur Funk, took us on a motor tour which took in Doulatabad and Sultanabad, Kum, Teheran, and Kasvin. We couldn't include Isfahan to my great regret, as Dr. Funk had to get back to his hospital. For years I longed to see that fabled city, of which the Persians say, "Half the world is Isfahan." (I achieved my desire in 1956 and found that it even surpassed my expectations. The glorious old buildings, the Maidan, the bridge across the river, were even more fabulous than I had anticipated, and the bazaars made me feel that I had stepped straight into the pages of the classic *Hajji Baba of Isfahan*.

After the Nairns opened the overland desert route from Baghdad to Syria and Lebanon, we went that way instead of making the long roundabout sea voyage which had been necessary before. Our first trip was in 1925; how happy I was to see Damascus, "the Pearl of the Desert" about which I had heard so much. After the long desert journey, it was easy to understand why the Prophet Mohammed said that Paradise would be a place of flowing streams. Then to Beirut, that lovely city by the sea, with the mountains behind it; it seemed to me then, and has done so ever since, like Paris, London, and New York, all in one.

We went by a Messagerie Maritime ship from Beirut to Naples, calling at Smyrna, Istanbul, and Athens. We had a tantalizing glimpse of the glamorous capital by the Bosphorus, and the children were especially intrigued by the Janissary Museum. Athens was a great experience for us and for the children; Alice, aged five, recalled in later years that she wore a red dress and picked poppies in the Theatre of Dionysus!

We saw Pompeii while we were at Naples; then went to Rome, a memorable experience because it was Holy Year; after that a pleasant sojourn in Switzerland, at Vevy and Geneva; a few days in Paris, and then a most enjoyable stay in Holland. In Leyden I took great satisfaction in showing my children the monument which commemorates the sojourn of the Pilgrim Fathers in the Netherlands, before they went to America. John was pleased to be able to say to me,

"Where would you have been, if your ancestors hadn't found a refuge in Holland?"

We discovered that the great Orientalist, Professor Snouck Hurgronjie, was in residence at the University of Leyden, and I urged my husband to go and call on him. At first he demurred, saying that he had no introductions and no formal clothes, that the professor would never have heard of him, and so on. His last feeble excuse was,

"What will you and the children do while I am there?"

I finally prevailed upon him and he had a very cordial welcome and a delightful call, which he described to us enthusiastically on his return. A neat Dutch maid opened the door to John and escorted him to the study, after he had sent in his card, and the Professor came out beaming and exclaimed,

"Welcome, Mynheer Van Ess! I am so happy to meet you! I have your Arabic grammars here on my shelf."

He was giving an examination in Arabic to a young man named Vander Meulen, who was about to go to Jidda in the

Netherlands Foreign Service, and he brushed his pupil off briskly, saying,

"You listen to me and Dr. Van Ess, and you will learn more than an examination can teach you."

They talked in Arabic and in Dutch, and discussed everything from weak verbs to the philosophy of the Muslim mystics, amply fortified by many cups of coffee.

Mr. Vander Meulen had a distinguished career in the Orient, and is the author of several books about his experiences in the Arab world. I met him years later, in Beirut and in Jerusalem, and he recalled his long ago meeting with my husband.

John greatly enjoyed talking Dutch during this visit to Holland; he had never lost his fluency and it pleased him to "surprise the natives." On a train journey, our fellow travellers in the compartment discussed us freely, as we were obviously an American family. They said the little girl was a "liefes Kind" (dear child) and looked like her mother, the boy was like his father; and how amazed they were when at length John leaned forward and said to one gentleman, in his best court Dutch,

"When you have finished with that newspaper, may I have a look at it?"

At a diamond cutting factory in Amsterdam, I got a hearty scolding because my children and I couldn't speak Dutch too!

We were also at a disadvantage in the long, long Sunday service in the *Groote Kerk*, where John was able to take in every detail with such deep appreciation and understanding. The children were greatly relieved when the preacher stopped his sermon and the congregation rose and sang a Dutch Psalm, but I almost had a mutiny on my hands when everyone sat down and the sermon resumed. We had to sit down again on the hard, narrow, straight-backed pews for at least another half hour.

We crossed from the Hook of Holland to Hull; the first morning in our hotel in London, the children came rushing in and said to us,

"The servants here can all speak English!"

After John and Alice were in school and college in America, their father and I took our vacations in Jerusalem or Lebanon. Palestine had a great deal to offer, and in the days before it was tragically divided we moved freely about in all parts of the Holy Land.

Such were our years of rich family living. We were often separated geographically—once we were in three different continents when Alice was in America, young John and I in France, and my husband in Iraq—but we were never separated in spirit. We were very happy in our private lives.

XIII
High Hope Goes On

Our schools under British military occupation and the Mandate were free to develop along the lines best suited to their needs. The girls' school had expanded so much that it required the full time of a single woman missionary without family responsibilities (and ultimately of two) as well as the staff of Arab teachers. I had regretfully severed my connection with it, while rejoicing in the success which made the change necessary.

My immediate successor was May DePree Thomas, who was shortly transferred to Baghdad to open a mission school for girls in the capital city.

For three decades after this, the Basrah girls' school was in the care of Charlotte Kellien and Rachel Jackson.

In 1930 a beautiful new girls' school plant was built in a large date-garden on the outskirts of the city. A spacious and adequate school building with ample playground areas and an attractive house for the "single ladies" were sheltered by a surrounding wall and met the needs in a Muslim community most acceptably.

The boys' school moved to the former hospital premises and a library and new recitation building were added and excellent facilities were developed for sports.

The boys' school curriculum led to a regular high school diploma which during that period was accepted by most American colleges. Many of our graduates went to American colleges and universities and most of them made good records. The courses of study were standard: history, mathematics, science and languages. Arabic was the language of instruction but English was taught so thoroughly that the boys who completed their schooling were all bi-lingual. The majority of the students were Muslims, but Bible classes were required, and John's classes in Christian ethics were among the most popular courses. The emphasis on character training was greatly appreciated by Arab parents.

In 1921 the policy was adopted of bringing an American

teacher, just out of college, for a three-year term. He taught English and sports, and was in charge of the boarding school or hostel, where he was guide, philosopher and friend to the boys under his care. The first of these, George Gosselink, later succeeded my husband as principal of the school. Our son, John Van Ess, Jr., came out as a short-termer in 1938.

The year 1927 marked the Silver Jubilee of John Van Ess' coming to Iraq, and a large group of leading members of the community wished to make a gift to the school in recognition and appreciation of his years of service to the Arabs. Their first suggestion was that he should have his portrait painted to be placed in the school. He deftly avoided this by telling them,

"We never put portraits of living persons in our schools, only after they are dead."

A science laboratory was chosen instead, the first of its kind in this part of the world, and its fame spread all over Iraq. A bronze inscription placed in the laboratory read:

As a momento of self-effacing service and loyalty. Presented by the people of Basrah in token of the services which Dr. John Van Ess, American missionary in Basrah, rendered in presenting knowledge and virtue for twenty-five years, and they have presented it to him for the use of his school on the occasion of Silver Jubilee that it may be our witness in the days to come of our appreciation thereof.

The most exciting item in the laboratory was a skeleton. The boys never tired of inspecting it, and people came from far and wide to see this curiosity. Before one large "At Home" when the laboratory was to be on view, the science teacher and the short-termer rigged up electric wires to the boney right hand of the skeleton, enough to give quite a shock to anyone who accepted their hospitable invitation to shake hands with it.

Sheikh Ahmed el Sabah, then the Ruler of Kuwait, was given a private showing of the laboratory on one of his visits to Basrah, and stood a long time contemplating the skeleton (not electrified this time). His comment was,

"H'm—dead!"

A few years later, Dr. Harold Storm asked for the loan of our Basrah skeleton, to be used in anatomy classes he was conducting for helpers in the mission hospital in Bahrain. Rachel Jackson was about to go down to Bahrain, and John asked her if she would mind escorting this unusual companion. Rachel, always ready to oblige, said,

"Well, I've never travelled with a skeleton before, but I suppose I can!"

She had to declare her effects at the Customs Office in Basrah before boarding the ship, and when she told them what was in the very long box in her freight, they inquired whether it was a scientific object or an antique.

The pattern followed in the boys' school during these years was of the ungraded classroom—groups rather than classes. Each boy recited in each subject where he would fit. Their graphs at first were wildly uneven, but as they learned how to study, or were stimulated by the desire to reach their friends of the same age or size, they would work harder on their weak subjects and gradually flatten out the graph. Each pupil was graphed on conduct as well as scholarship, and earned privileges or penalties as the case demanded. This system, though developed independently, corresponded with the most modern theories of progressive education then being evolved in America.

Dr. Paul Monroe, principal of Teachers' College in New York City, visited Iraq in 1932 at the request of the Minister of Education. He was asked to draw up a plan for the whole educational system of Iraq, and made an extended tour of the country. He was an old friend of John's, and we were delighted to welcome him when he came to Basrah. He inspected our schools throughly, and when John asked him for a frank appraisal of the School of High Hope, he said with a sigh of envy,

"You have had a unique opportunity to develop a progressive school under ideal conditions. I find nothing to criticize and everything to praise."

The students at this time came from families of every class of society: sheikhs, old-fashioned religious leaders, up-to-date merchants, government officials, landowners, army officers, clerks in offices, carpenters, policemen, sign painters, shop keepers, farmers—and from villages as well as from the town. The sons of the paramount sheikh of all the confederated tribes on the Euphrates, the Muntafiq, were in the boarding school, and several came from other ruling families in the region.

At the close of the war there had been a realignment of

mission work, and we now had as colleagues in the north of Iraq the members of the United Mission in Mesopotamia, established in 1923. Co-operating in this were the Presbyterian Church (North, and South), the United Presbyterian Church and the Reformed Church in America. (Later known as the United Mission in Iraq, it is now the Iraq Fellowship.) Work was carried on in Baghdad, Hillah, Mosul, and for a time in Dohuk, in Kurdistan.

A flourishing YMCA in Baghdad had an effective educational and cultural program, and maintained a comfortable hostel where we often used to stay when we went through the capital city.

With the termination of the Mandate in October, 1932, and national independence attained, the Iraqi government naturally set up its own standards of education, with which all schools had to conform. In 1936 provisions were introduced in the conscription law exempting young men from military service only if they were pupils in schools, and then only if in due course they passed the examinations scheduled by the Department of Education. The mission school was therefore obliged to follow the government curriculum exactly. (This bore no resemblance to the counsels of perfection drawn up by Dr. Monroe.)

Because of the superior momentum and prestige of the state schools, sons of the well-to-do flocked to them, especially since the professions of law, medicine, and teaching, and all higher government posts were subsequently to be open only to their graduates.

It is not the function of mission schools to parallel or compete with government institutions, so the manifest opportunity at this point lay in capitalizing on what missionaries are supposed to possess in unique measure—dedicated personalities and Christian motivation, neither of which a government can buy or command.

The state schools had neither room nor appeal for the boys of the underprivileged classes which make up the greater part of the population, so the mission decided to specialize in that group. The results were very gratifying. The pupils, many of them from the villages, were vigorous, simple in their tastes, accustomed to hardship, eager and approachable. A fair number of well-to-do Arabs who were independent in their thinking continued to send their sons to the School of High Hope, because of the superior teaching of English and the good moral atmosphere.

In 1940 we had a crisis in our schools. Nationalism had developed a definite anti-Western bias, and Iraq decided to follow the example of Turkey and Iran, and unify and standardize the whole educational system on strict nationalist lines. A new law was passed forbidding all primary school pupils to attend foreign or private schools. Restrictions were also placed on the teaching of certain subjects in secondary schools, except by teachers directly appointed by the Department of Education. This would have wiped out our girls' school in Basrah entirely, as it had only the primary grades, and seriously affected the School of High Hope, and the mission school for girls in Baghdad. It also hit the Jesuit School in Baghdad, and the long-established schools there and in Basrah maintained by Roman Catholic Sisters. John went to Baghdad in the summer of 1940 to consult and protest, and was asked to be the spokesman to the government for all the private schools concerned.

A working agreement was reached by which the schools functioned as before, and our mission schools were registered in the name of the Protestant Arab Evangelical Congregation. This happy outcome was achieved largely through the good offices of Nuri Pasha Said, my husband's loyal friend throughout the years, and who had been many times Prime Minister of Iraq.

Mutual relationships with government authorities were thenceforth friendly and cordial, and immediately after the threatened crisis was resolved, the enrollment in all departments was the largest in the history of the school. The morale of the boys was excellent, and they were to play a worthy part in the stirring events of May, 1941.

XIV

The Mission and World War II

In the fall of 1938 the new short-termer for the School of High Hope was our son, John Van Ess, Jr. He had graduated from Princeton in June, and the Arab world in which he was born made a strong appeal to him. He was offered several attractive positions in the United States, but he decided that he wanted to come back to Basrah. He had studied Arabic at Princeton, as part of his modern language course, and on his return to Iraq his fluency in speaking soon came back.

He reorganized the English courses in the high school, and built up a strong athletic program. His presence was a great joy to his father and me personally, and it was a moral support to have our son with us during the various crises which occurred in the next eventful years.

The political climate in Iraq was increasingly anti-British during the years just before World War II. After the Arab rebellion in Palestine in 1936, many of the leaders found asylum in Baghdad. Young Syrians who resented French control in their country also went to Iraq, where they became teachers or found other forms of employment. Young Iraqi intellectuals had an emotional resentment against the British, dating back to the Mandate, and carrying over into suspicion of the Anglo-Iraq Treaty which came into force in 1932, when Iraq became a member of the League of Nations.

International tensions in Europe were increasing with the rising power of the Nazis, and both Germans and Italians in Baghdad exploited the situation. They joined with the exiled leaders of the Palestinian rebellion to stir up hatred against the British, both by political activities and by influencing the Iraqi Army with their propaganda. German, Italian, and Japanese business interests penetrated the Iraqi economy and made rapid progress.

In October, 1939, the famous Mufti of Jerusalem, Haj Ameen el Husseini, who had been the leader of the rebellion of Palestinian Arabs, came to Baghdad. His prestige was immense, and his skill at intrigue was just what the anti-British factions welcomed and utilized to the full.

There followed a very uneasy period in our little country. One amusing event occurred, in which my husband was directly concerned.

The aide-de-camp of a powerful Indian Maharajah appeared one day and asked John if it would be convenient for his master to come to call next day. John replied that he would be honored, and accordingly on the morrow the great man arrived, with several aides, in a Cadillac car. Young John was present (I was away) and one of the aides said to him,

"Won't you show us your garden, Mr. Van Ess, while the Maharajah talks to your father?"

So the two seniors were left alone, and after tea and the usual polite conversation, the Maharajah got down to his real business.

Dr. Van Ess, perhaps you have heard that my beloved wife, the Maharanee, has just recovered from a critical illness. I vowed to Allah while she was so ill, that I would make a large thank-offering if she recovered. There are two shrines to which I should like to award these gifts [and he mentioned two world-famous Shiah Muslim shrines in Iraq] and I should like your advice as to what to give them. You have lived here so long, I am sure you know the religious sheikhs who are in charge of these shrines, better than I do. What do you think that they would consider a worthy gift?

John thought for a while, and then came up with a suggestion.

Your Highness, why not give each of these shrines a handsome crystal chandelier, to show your gratitude to Allah for the restoration to health of your beautiful Maharanee? I think if you gave the larger shrine a chandelier that cost fifty thousand pounds, and the smaller, one worth thirty thousand, that it would be a suitable and worthy gift, acceptable to the religious sheikhs.

With this, and many parting salutations and expressions of mutual esteem and goodwill, the distinguished guest took his departure, gathering up his escort in the garden.

What John knew, and the Maharajah knew that he knew, but never hinted at by the flicker of an eyelid, was that the Germans were trying to get the religious sheikhs to incite the local tribes, whom they controlled, to revolt against Britain. He wanted John's advice as to how much money it would take to keep them on the Allied side of the war.

A few weeks later, the Maharajah called again, with his entourage, and the same ceremonious procedure was carried out. After tea and pleasant conversation, the guest thanked John profusely for his advice.

I fulfilled my vow, my dear sir, and carried out your advice with one exception. I feared that the religious sheikhs in charge of the smaller shrine might feel slighted if they received a lesser sum than I gave to the other, so I gave each holy place fifty thousand pounds for a chandelier. I hope you approve.

John assented gravely, and agreed that it was a wise decision. The Maharajah took his leave, with many compliments, and left a gold cigarette case for my husband and a silver case for young John.

There was no revolt among those tribes and needless to say no chandeliers. In after years, when John was free to tell the story, he used to say,

"Was I right, to advise spending one hundred thousand pounds of Allied money as a bribe to keep those tribes from joining the Germans?"

At the end of January, 1941, I left the two Johns to take care of each other and carry on the school, and began a long wartime journey to the USA. I had promised Alice that somehow or other, war or no war, I would get to America in plenty of time to see her graduate from Mount Holyoke College in June. I travelled to Bombay on a British India ship, and from there to New York on the "President Taylor," all the way around South Africa and up the long stretches of the Atlantic Ocean. I reached my own country in time to spend the spring in New England, which had never been more lovely.

It was comforting to be in such a beautiful place, and close to relatives and friends, for the war news was very bad, especially in the Near East. I watched the newspapers with painful interest to see what was developing in Iraq, and listened constantly to broadcasts on the radio.

Early in 1941, an official from the German Foreign Office had arrived in Damascus and begun a vigorous Nazi campaign. He announced that the German army was invincible and would soon reach Syria, and that Iraq would join Germany, and so would Afghanistan. Persia was already co-operating with the Nazis. Then India would revolt against the British.

This encouraged the anti-Ally element in Baghdad, who had been reinforced by the Mufti and other exiled Palestinian leaders, and in April a *coup d'etat* was successfully carried out. Rashid Ali el Gailani, who had several times been a member of the Iraqi cabinet, seized power, backed by a military group of four generals who were called The Golden Square. The Regent, Amir Abdul Ilah, who was the uncle of the boy King Feisal the Second, escaped from Iraq and was followed by Nuri Pasha Said, Jemil Pasha Medfai, and other senior Iraqi officials who were firmly pro-British. Rashid Ali's rebel government announced that the regent was deposed.

Britain thereupon sent a brigade of troops by sea to Basrah, a measure within the terms of the Anglo-Iraq Treaty, which also allowed the British two air bases in Iraq. When this news was made public in the newspapers of America, my friends all said to me,

"You must be relieved to know that British troops are in Iraq," and I replied,

"I am not in the least relieved—the government now in power would be delighted to have the Germans arrive, and all would be peaceful, but if the British send armed forces there, I know that there will be a clash."

On the second day of May I was in Grand Central Station, returning to New England after a visit to my sister in Virginia, and to my horror I saw headlines in all the papers on the newsstands, announcing "War In Iraq." For a month the news was fragmentary and contradictory, and I was frantic worrying about John and Young John, and the Gosselinks and our other colleagues in Basrah, as well as all our English friends.

It was announced a few days later that the Nazis were in Iraq. Our mission headquarters in New York tried to cable to Basrah but got no reply; then they were in touch with the State Department in Washington but they couldn't get any direct news either.

One newspaper said that there had been heavy fighting near Basrah, "especially in Liwa." Now "liwa" is not a proper noun, it is the word for a district, and this didn't make any more sense than if one said there was trouble in Chicago, especially in "county."

At last at the end of May we received the welcome news that the British had occupied Baghdad and that everyone was safe.

Eventually we heard what had happened. After the first British troops had been landed, in April, the Rashid Ali group in Baghdad informed the British Embassy that they would not allow any more to come into Iraq. There was already another convoy on the way which did in the course of time land. Meanwhile the Vichy Government in Syria had been ordered to give all possible assistance to German aircraft passing through on their way to Iraq, and to allow them to use Syrian aerodromes. A further order said, "English aircraft must be attacked by all possible means."

The Germans sent munitions of war to Mosul and Baghdad by train, and sent their fighting planes to bomb British air bases in Iraq. German advisers and staff officers were sent to Baghdad by air. German aircraft were operating from Osul and Irbil. If Hitler had not been slowed up six weeks in Greece and Crete by unexpected British resistance, Nazi troops would have been sent to Iraq, and the outcome might have been different. There was hard fighting for a month, and many losses, before the rebel forces capitulated. Rashid Ali and his Golden Square fled to Persia, as did the Mufti of Jerusalem and Herr Grobba, the German minister in Iraq.

The pro-Ally leaders returned to Baghdad with the regent and a new constitutional government was formed, and the country settled down again.

John and the others of our group in Basrah had been in the midst of the fray. Jails had been opened to allow the prisoners to join the rebels. At one time there were Gurkha soldiers of the British Expeditionary Force guarding the bridge just below our mission compound, and rebels on the other side, so our school was literally between two fires. John acted as a go-between, organized an informal city council, and posted high school boys at strategic points to help keep order. I fear that they, and my son John, rather enjoyed all the excitement.

The school re-opened with a record enrollment and enhanced prestige, and finished the school year with a flourish.

John Jr. remained in the Arab world, briefly in Saudi Arabia and then with the American Military Mission in Iraq.

John then left for America, journeying in the opposite way from the one I had taken. My husband travelled on a Dutch ship by way of the Pacific, which he thoroughly enjoyed. The officers were delighted to have an American passenger who spoke their language, and took him ashore with them to their clubs at all the Far East ports. At the ship's banquet in honor of the birthday of the Queen of the Netherlands, he was asked to make a speech, which he considered a great honor.

He joined Alice and me at the end of August and we went to live in Princeton for the winter. We were there on that fateful Sunday afternoon of the seventh of December, when Japan attacked Pearl Harbor.

We had felt so closely identified with the Allied cause during the previous two years in Basrah, that it seemed quite natural to us for our own country to be one of the Allies now.

Early in the New Year John was greatly concerned at the publication in the New York Times of January 5, 1942, of a plan for an all-Jewish Army to fight the Axis powers, entitled "Jews Fight for the Right to Fight." It had an impressive list of sponsors, several of them non-Jewish, and appeared to have the blessing of Secretary Stimson himself. John corresponded vigorously with officials in the State Department, expressing his misgivings about the damage such a project would do to American relations with all the Arab countries. Other Americans familiar with conditions in the Near East did the same, and the plan was never carried out.

One of the sponsors was Mary E. Woolley, the former President of Mount Holyoke College. John and I were having dinner with her in New York at just the time when the Jewish Army was being discussed. In the course of the evening my husband said courteously,

"Miss Woolley, I should very much like to know how you came to give your endorsement to this undertaking."

She explained to him the strong case presented to her by Jewish authorities, and her readiness to have her name used in what sounded to her like a good cause. He questioned her tactfully to see how much she knew of the whole Palestine problem—the different types of Jews involved, and the wide disagreement between extreme Zionists and such leaders as Dr.

Magnes. She listened with deep attention and interest, asked John very searching questions, and after he had given her a thorough briefing in the whole situation, she said decidedly.

"I shall instruct my secretary tomorrow to have my name taken off the list of sponsors. I am very grateful to you, Mr. Van Ess, for giving me all this information. I've never heard that side of the case before."

Late in January, the State Department asked my husband if he would consider making a trip to the rulers of the Arab countries as a special envoy of the president, to "foster mutual understanding"—in other words, to try to get the Arabs to stay on the Allied side during the war, or at least to remain neutral, in spite of German pressure and German successes. The plan was never carried out, owing to what the State Department said were "insuperable difficulties." John wrote them on February 17, 1942:

I am immensely relieved, for with an all-out German offensive almost certain to occur in the Near East very soon, it would have been totally impossible to collect any stable Arab opinion. They are, and would be, jittery, and would want to wait and see the result. And as for propaganda, the best pro-Ally propaganda is victories, or at least manifest progress in that direction.

The progress was slow, and when Rommel was less than one hundred miles from Alexandria, the prospects seemed very dark.

We moved to New York City in May, 1942, to a pleasant apartment on Morningside Drive, owned by Columbia University. As the Navy was using many of the university buildings for training their recruits, including the Waves, we were warm and comfortable all the following winter and had no problems of fuel rationing, since the government maintained the university heating plant. Alice and I were both working in New York, and it seemed advisable to establish ourselves for what might be an indefinite stay in America.

John was busy with writing and lecturing, and with conferences with the State Department. Some of our Jesuit friends from Baghdad were studying Arabic at Columbia, and used to come around for special supplementary sessions with my husband. He had many Jewish friends, and often young rabbis from the Jewish seminary near us came in for discussions. When

I got home from my office late in the afternoon, I might see half a dozen soft black felt hats on the hall table, and never knew whether I would find Jesuits or rabbis having tea with John in the living room.

In January, 1943, the heaviest blow of our lives befell us. Our son John, Jr. was in Basrah, working with the American Military Mission now established there, and he died suddenly within a few days of his twenty-sixth birthday. He had been recruiting officer for local labor, and his facility in Arabic and his knowledge of the people of Basrah made him invaluable in this capacity. He worked under great pressure and was no doubt careless about his health, and succumbed to a combination of tropical diseases.

When you lose a child, something of yourself dies too. You are never complete again. I felt utterly hollow, and I used to wonder why people who met me didn't say,

"Why, Mrs. Van Ess, you are nothing but a shell! What has happened to you?"

John's health had been indifferent for a long time, and he never recovered from the shock of this great sorrow. The mystical qualities of his faith developed strongly, and the borderline between this world and the next became very faint. His great affirmation was that time and eternity are one and that life is continuous and progressive. My mother had held this belief strongly too, especially during the last years of her life. She and John had been much alike in their sensitive spiritual perceptions, and it fortified me to have their unshaken and unshakable Christian faith as an influence and an example.

It was an inestimable comfort to have our daughter with us at this time, and we were fortunate in having work to occupy us. I was acting as executive secretary to the Women's Department of the Board of Foreign Missions of the Reformed Church in America, and it was an absorbing and exacting job. We were deeply involved with the war effort and in the happenings all around the world. Orphan Missions, Church World Service, and relief work of many sorts, were in full swing. I sat on many interdenominational committees and attended many conferences. My own personal grief was gathered in with the sorrows of the world, and the epic quality of those war years made it an ennobling experience.

John at once embarked on a writing project which John, Jr. had been urging him for a long time to undertake. This was a book about the Arabs. We had been struck by the fact that while there was a great deal of propaganda in America for the Jews, there was practically none for the Arabs. Few people knew anything about them; they had no organization and no spokesman. John called his book *Meet the Arab*, and it was published by the John Day Company in October, 1943.

It gave a brief history of the Arabs; there was a chapter on their religion, and another on their language and literature. The Bedouin, the marsh Arabs, and different minorities were all vividly described, and leading personalities in the Arab world aptly characterized. John wrote it in an informal style and included many of his own experiences. Throughout the book he expressed both directly and indirectly his high regard for the Arabs and his appreciation of their friendship. For his chapter on women, entitled "Fatima and Her Sisters," he used the articles I had written for *Asia* magazine, since his only knowledge of Arab women was what I could tell him, and he thought it advisable to let me speak for myself. The last part of the book dwelt on the future, and the importance of the Arab countries in the world after the war. He offered his solution for Palestine, and his fervent hope for a peaceful settlement which would do justice to both Arabs and Jews.

Meet the Arab had very favorable reviews; in later years, the United Nations organizations put it on their list of recommended reading for all personnel going to the Near East. As late as 1960, I was told by a graduate student at Columbia University, who was doing his Ph.D. thesis in linguistics, that the chapter in *Meet the Arab* called "The Language of the Angels" was the most valuable single exposition he had found on his subject.

The book was also subsequently published in England, and was greatly enjoyed and appreciated by our British friends.

By this time we were longing to return to Basrah. The Axis forces in North Africa had been defeated in May, 1943, and the tide seemed to have turned. The Middle East felt reassured that the outcome of the war would be victory for the Allies. The State Department was anxious to have my husband back in Iraq, and would have given him a passport and passage priority much earlier. However, for a time no American civilian women were permitted to travel in that area, and our Board doctors were not willing to have John go without me to look after him. When the world situation improved, we renewed our efforts to get passports for both of us, and these were granted in the fall of 1943.

Alice had been wishing for months to join the Waves, and had only refrained because she didn't want to leave us alone. She went into uniform at the same time that we left the country.

We sailed from Philadelphia to Lisbon in November on a Portuguese ship, which was brightly lighted at night since it was neutral. Several times as we crossed the Atlantic Ocean we got out of the way to allow Allied convoys to pass us; when this happened at night, it was deeply moving to see the long line of ghostly ships sailing silently through the starlit darkness, to their unknown destinations. At Lisbon we were fortunate enough to get passage in a few days, on another Portuguese ship which took us around the coast of Africa and up the east coast to Lourenco Marques, in Mozambique. Here we received a cable from our daughter, saying that she had finished her training at midshipman's school and had now received her commission as ensign in the Naval Reserve, which made us very happy for her.

In Lourenco Marques we were fortunate again, in contrast to many of our American and British friends, some of whom had been waiting for months to get on their way to India, or via India to Chungking. We were lucky enough to be accepted by the captain of an English freighter under the War Shipping Board, who was taking coal to the Mediterranean. We were signed on as crew, and each given one shilling for our pay when we disembarked at Suez. We had with us a young man, Harry Almond, going to Basrah as a short-termer in the School of High Hope, and he had done a good deal of sailing and really made himself useful on the voyage. Belle Bogard, bound for our mission school in Baghdad, was put down as a stewardess and so was I. The blackout every night was a trial, but it was a joy to be with English officers and men, and to listen to the news from England every night on the radio.

At Mombasa, the port of Kenya, we joined a convoy of fifteen ships escorted by two corvettes. It was a motley assortment, and one little Greek cargo ship was constantly dropping behind and slowing down the whole convoy. It was amusing to see one of the little corvettes swing around and try to hurry her up, like a shepherd dog rounding up straggling sheep. One day we saw two whales, one of whom spouted the whole length of the convoy. From Suez we went to Cairo by train, and friends in the Army Transport Corps arranged comfortable railway accommodation for us to Haifa, **where we joined a motor convoy bound for Baghdad.**

XV

Home Again in Basrah

A letter of mine to friends in America described our homecoming to Basrah thus:

We arrived at our destination after our long journey. All our colleagues were at the station to meet us, and such a large group of "Old Boys" and other Arab friends, as well as several English ones, that we were quite literally overwhelmed. Since then my husband has had one constant stream of callers, of every class of society, and the warmth and sincerity of their welcome makes us appreciate how glad they are of our return. Two formal programs of welcome were held as soon as J.V.E. was able to "take" them, one for the present students and one for former pupils and friends of the school. My feminine friends all sent word to know when they might come to see me—it takes a little arranging for these ladies who have to observe "purdah"—so I have been receiving them every Friday afternoon and have had all my oldest and dearest friends in my home. I have lived continuously in Basrah for thirty-three years, except for furloughs, and my husband one term before that, so you can't wonder that it seems home to us as does no other place in the world. Our house is lovely. When the YMCA personnel vacated it (a succession of them have been using it in our absence), they secured color-wash for the walls, and George Gosselink had it all fixed up, all our things in place; and the women of the station, including Ruth Jackson and Cornelia Dalenberg, who were visiting here, got everything arranged so that it was ready for us to step right into. We can never express our appreciation for all they did. The garden is at its very best at this time of the year and the flowerbeds are a blaze of color, hollyhocks and oleanders coming into blossom, and the trees full of bulbuls—Persian nightingales. Some of you know how I feel about living in a city, and will pardon this lyric outburst. After several years in New York City, it goes to my head to be in a house surrounded with green and space and flowers. Also it's a joy for me to have my own things again.

I have resumed my club work, which has gone forward with great vigor under Mrs. Gosselink's leadership. She has had Rachel Jackson to help her; fortunately Rachel and I overlapped by a week.

The little king of this country paid a visit to our city this month, and I was invited to a select tea-party to meet the Queen Mother—the widow of the young King Ghazi, who was killed in a motor accident about five years ago. The chief interest of these gatherings is looking over one's fellow guests. I saw many old friends and acquaintances. J.V.E.'s book has aroused great interest here, and is to be translated into Arabic shortly. So far the only chapter that has been translated, and appeared in an abridged form in a vernacular paper, is mine about the women.

I am very much pleased to find that the young women of the privileged classes are taking to opportunities for study, and are attending discussion groups, held in connection with organizations which have been formed in this country since it became our ally. Different members of our mission have cooperated in various ways, and as soon as I am more settled—figuratively as well as literally (I am the latter), I am going to see if that will not provide me with the opportunity I have been wishing for, for many years, to reach this group otherwise than merely socially.

I have attended one of our "At Homes" in our girls' school in Basrah City, and saw many old friends, and old pupils of my own from the days when I was in school work all the time.

The whole group of Arab Christian women had their weekly meeting with Mrs. Gosselink and me on Wednesday, and a tea party on the lawn afterwards. So, you see, I am gathering up the threads of my life here and finding it very satisfying and comforting to do so. The sympathy and affection of all these friends has helped us both greatly, in returning and encountering all the associations of our family life. We feel our son's presence in this place he loved so well, and know this is where he would wish us to be.

It amuses me now, to see how obviously this letter was written with one eye on the censor.

The Arab Christian women, to whom I referred, were members of the Oriental churches. From early days our mission had not converts from Islam, but "born Christians," descendants of one of the minorities in Asiatic Turkey who had never become Muslims. There was a strong group in the Arabic speaking area around Mardin who had become Protestants, due to the influence of the Congregational missionaries who worked with members of the Oriental churches. From early days our Mission had secured teachers, evangelists, and hospital helpers from the excellent schools and colleges in Mardin and Aintab. As time went on, relatives and friends joined them in Iraq, especially in the period immediately after World War I when Turkey was in a most unsettled state. Eventually there was a large congregation in Basrah, and they built their own church and had their own pastor. They won an honorable place in the community; the doctors, pharmacists, midwives, lawyers, teachers of both sexes and business men had a high reputation for integrity and good citizenship.

Their church was entirely independent of the mission, but we joined them in their worship services, and for many years I was the president of their women's society, to be succeeded by Christine Gosselink.

This Christian fellowship was a valued feature of our lives, and some of the older women are among my dearest friends.

Basrah was now an important military and naval base, a supply depot for Allied forces in the area; and the port which forwarded all the Lend Lease material for Russia, by the land route through Persia. If Rommel had captured North Africa and the Suez Canal, the main line of defense for the Allies would have been just west of us. The British air base at Shaiba had become an enormous armed camp, and there was a large American base at Khoramshahr, down the river on the Persian side. This had an excellent military hospital with the latest equipment (I once had an infected tooth extracted there), and there was another one at the base up near Ahwaz.

Basrah was full of men in uniform, and we kept continuous open house, chiefly for American and British officers and men. We had our own work to carry on, and it was a busy and absorbing life.

John had asked to be relieved of the administration of the school, so George Gosselink continued as principal. My husband taught classes regulary in Arabic, on Young Men's Problems, The Good Teacher, and other subjects which related to religion and character. He did a great deal of personal work, which **he** described thus:

My main effort has been expended on meeting people in my home. They have come in large numbers, and indeed among those who came to welcome me to Basrah were some who never before had darkened our doors, and who had in fact been definitely hostile to our work, though not to me personally. Particularly gratifying were the visits of numbers of former pupils, most of whom are now lucratively employed.

In December, 1944, I described our life as follows:

The weather is completely winter now; we had lots of rain and it turned cold all at once. I hate summer and I love winter and feel like a new person, but even *I* could do with a little central heating. Our bathroom is 56° in the morning. But we have two oil heaters that are very efficient, lots of wood for the open fires and plenty of warm clothes. I have been giving out the warm garments from my Roseland Guild box—a long and often disheartening job. All the club girls, big and little (over 100) are easy because they are enrolled; but the women, babies, and former girls need a lot of sorting out to be sure the neediest get the things. Christine Gosselink and children are back from school in India, and we waited and celebrated Thanksgiving at the later date so they'd be with us. I had to ransack the whole Near East to get cinnamon for my pumpkin pies. A Red Cross worker, Margaret Conant, from our base in Khoramshahr, finally came to my rescue. She had spent a weekend with us recently. We have a lot of Americans in here, first and last, army and navy, and it's such a pleasure. I see a lot of British servicemen at the canteen where I work every Saturday evening. The other afternoon I came in and found three U. S. boys—one Amherst man, one Harvard, and one a naturalized Russian, and so interesting—all talking religion with John as hard as they could. They overlapped with dinner guests, an English colonel and a Welsh chaplain. Our own padre came in to see me on canteen business, and it was a great combination.

I have been doing a great deal of calling lately; Arab friends, both rich and poor, the former both the old-fashioned and conservative, and the new-fangled and progressive. I visited the Government High School for Girls this week. I always like to know what they are doing. Those few privileged girls should be the hope for the future. The new president of the Iraqi Senate, a life-long friend of John's, has an old-fashioned family which I went to see last week. They were all in Arab dress in a great big room with lovely rugs, narrow mattresses and pillows around the walls, and nothing else except a big charcoal brazier in the middle of the room. I am always so glad that I have known that era, it has so much color and charm.

The next day I went to tea at "Public Relations" and saw a group of progressives. One was a pupil of mine thirty years ago as a young girl. I haven't seen her since her marriage, twenty years ago. She has been with her husband to Geneva, Paris, Teheran, and other places (he is in the Iraq Diplomatic Service) and has developed into a lovely gracious woman. We were so happy to meet again and fell on each other's necks. She's down from the capital for a short visit to relatives.

The day before, our old Zahra had all the mission family to an Arab meal on our servants' compound, to celebrate the Gosselink children's return. We sat on the floor in the "Evangelistic Hut" (a term that amuses Harry Almond immensely) where I have my Thursday meetings. We ate with our fingers, and all enjoyed ourselves thoroughly.

One very disappointing event occurred that year, which John took greatly to heart.

He had sent a copy of *Meet the Arab* to Nuri Said, as soon as it was published in 1943. The pasha was very much pleased with it, and upon our return to Iraq, he asked my husband to have the book translated into Arabic for publication. This task occupied John and one of his teachers throughout the summer of 1944. When it was finished, it was sent to Baghdad for the approval of the chief censor and director of propaganda. In the meantime, Nuri and his cabinet had been replaced by another set of leaders, fiercely nationalistic, and unsympathetic to any recognition of Western influence or Western friendships. The censor refused to allow the book to be published in Arabic, and issued an order that the edition in English of *Meet the Arab* should be prohibited and all copies in Iraq confiscated. (Needless to say, black market copies were in great demand and fetched astronomical prices.)

The reasons given for this action, which would have been ludicrous if the result had not been so unhappy, were points to be picked up by anyone who answered the description of a "hypersensitive super-patriot." They were: 1) a statement that "If Mohammed was a prophet, as some historians affirm . . ."

was interpreted as denying that Mohammed was a prophet; 2) unfavorable remarks about King Hussein of the Hejaz, the father of King Feisal the First; 3) favorable mention of Ibn Saud, King of Saudi Arabia, the successful rival of the founder of the Iraq royal family. Resentment was felt because his picture, in the group of illustrations in the banned book, came before that of King Feisal.

This action hurt John very deeply, and his physical energy was so low that he had lost some of his emotional resilience. He found it hard to look at it dispassionately, and appraise it with his mind and not his feelings. It was petty politics on the part of a small fanatic group, and had no relation whatever to the personal esteem and affection with which he was regarded by his Arab friends throughout Iraq. The ban was lifted shortly before his death in 1949, when Nuri was again prime minister.

In 1946 we had the happiness of a long visit from our daughter, who was released from active service in the Waves that spring. In spite of floods which inundated our property, killed all our vegetation except the date palms, and obliged us to go about our compound by boat, we had a most happy summer. Alice enjoyed visiting the scenes of her childhood, and all our Arab friends were delighted to welcome her back to the land of her birth.

The next year she came back to the Near East in a civilian capacity, and was on the staff of the American Consulate in Dharan, Saudi Arabia. This gave her an opportunity to spend Christmas with us in Basrah in 1947, and to get frequent unexpected rides to Basrah when an air force or oil company plane was making a trip.

In the summer of 1948 she was transferred to the American Embassy in Beirut, and her father and I went to Brummanna, in the mountains of Lebanon above Beirut, for our vacation, since we could not go to Jerusalem because of the troubled political conditions. Our daughter's fate awaited her there in Beirut, as I had found mine so many years ago in Bahrain. She met William Dodd Brewer, a young Foreign Service officer, who had been sent to Beirut by the State Department for his first overseas assignment, and they became engaged and were married in Basrah the following January. He was a New Englander and a graduate of Williams College, with a family background similar to mine, and he had a flair for politics which made him very congenial to his future father-in-law.

Their wedding was of deepest interest to all our friends in Basrah, Arabs as well as Europeans, and to the whole mission. A good number of our colleagues travelled from other stations of the mission to be present. The ceremony took place in St. Peter's Church, which we had attended since Alice was a small child. Her father was strong enough to walk the whole length of the church aisle with his daughter on his arm, and to give her away at the right moment in the beautiful Anglican service, which gave him deep satisfaction.

Our retirement was facing us in a few months time, and the thing closest to John's heart, after Alice's happiness and well-being, was the School of High Hope.

This was now well-established in the community, and had pursued a comparatively uneventful course ever since 1940. At the time of the Palestinian crisis, with the strong anti-American feeling following our government's recognition of Israel, there were no demonstrations against us or our schools, nor any attempt to boycott us. At the order of students of some other schools, a few of our boys joined in a very lukewarm way in "token" strikes and demonstrations, but these were negligible.

George Gosselink was an experienced and capable principal, and the current short-termer, Jake Holler, was a worthy successor to a long line of outstanding predecessors.

From the early years of World War II, a young men's club, subsequently known as the Royal Union Athletic Club, used a building on our mission compound. They enlarged it considerably at their own expense, with the understanding that it would eventually revert to the mission. This club, which was cultural and philanthropic as well as athletic, had as its nucleus chiefly young men who had graduated from our school, and who were now in professional life, government service, or in business. They maintained a night school which used our buildings, and opened two or more in other parts of town. Several similar social and athletic clubs branched off from this one, which later occupied very fine premises not far from the mission.

Our school had its own social center, with varying activities suited to the different seasons. The basketball court was floodlit and was used extensively by many organizations besides our own school teams.

A list of "Old Boys" compiled at about this time showed doctors, lawyers, teachers, pharmacists, dentists, merchants, oil company officials and employees, and many tradesmen and craftsmen. In government employ were army and air force officers; Port Directorate officials and river pilots; officials and clerks in the Departments of Customs, Justice, Education, Agriculture, Antiquities, Railways, on the Water Board and the Date Board, in the Bureau of Orphans, and in the Criminal Investigation Department (the equivalent of the FBI).

Several were members of the Chamber of Deputies in Baghdad; others were in Iraqi embassies and consulates abroad. One was for years the Iraqi member of the International Commission of Civil Aviation. Another succeeded his father as paramount sheikh of all the confederated Arabs on the Euphrates. Some of these served with distinction, and practically all with credit.

Many changes had taken place in the Near East with the discovery of oil and the great industrial developments it brought. Mechanistic and materialistic thinking greatly affected the old patterns and standards of behavior. Airlines crisscrossed Iraq, bringing all parts of the world unbelievably close. Nationalistic fervor looked toward the future viewing the past of this ancient land with indifference or impatience.

John could well look back with humble pride at the long and checkered history of the school and what it had contributed in the past. Now he recognized the challenge of the present, and the opportunity of his successors to train constructive leadership for the future. He justly had high hopes for the years to come.

His health was deteriorating rapidly, and the cardiac asthma from which he had suffered for some years made him almost immobile. It seemed as though after Alice's marriage he had relaxed, and had given up the effort to be active physically. His brain was sharper than ever, perhaps as compensation for his bodily weakness, and he thoroughly enjoyed teaching his classes, which now came to our house and met in his study. He worked steadily on his last book, called in English *Living Issues*, a comprehensive summary of his courses on Young Men's Problems, which his students had urged him to prepare for publication. A former student came down from Baghdad to help him finish it, and from his bed, a few days before the date set for our departure from Basrah, John dictated the last words of the Arabic original.

There were many farewell gatherings: the "Old Boys," the present student body, the British community, and the Arab Evangelical Church, each gave us a party. There were speeches expressing heartfelt appreciation for our years of service to the Arabs, and we received many charming gifts of "Presentation Silver." The large silver salver given us by the British community, with all their names engraved on the back, was considered by the Sabean silversmith who made it to be the finest piece of work he had ever done. It had bunches of gold dates on the sides, and appropriate Basrah scenes inlaid in black on the corners.

Two days before we were to leave Basrah, in the early hours before dawn, John Van Ess quietly stopped breathing. His students all said,

"It was never meant that he should leave us."

With love and reverence they carried his coffin on their shoulders all the way from our house to St. Peter's Church, where his funeral service took place; and again from the gates of the British War Cemetery to the far corner where the plot for civilians lies. In Arab fashion the bearers "spelled" each other, so that present school boys and former students all had a chance to perform this last service to their well-loved teacher and friend. He was buried close to the grave of our son John, which was just what he would have wished.

As I thought of his free spirit soaring away in the dawn, after the long months of shortened breath and failing strength, this verse filled my mind:

"They that wait upon the Lord shall renew their strength; they shall mount up with wings as eagles; they shall run and not be weary; and they shall walk, and not faint."

XVI

Politics, Palestine and Personality

In one of the travel documents carried by John Van Ess while touring in desert and marshes as a young man, he was described as "a tall harmless monk." Tall he certainly was; harmless from the point of view of the Turkish officials who issued his papers, because he represented no military, political or business interests. A "monk," though inaccurate, showed that they recognized the fact that his life was motivated by his religious convictions.

John had a deep interest in politics for as long as he could remember. He knew the names of the American secretaries of state and British prime ministers well back into the nineteenth century and in many cases some of the members of their cabinets. He had a very strong sense of history and of course when he went to the Near East he became particularly concerned with the Arab countries and Turkey and their relation to the rest of the world.

He took a keen interest in the changes which occurred in the Turkish Empire after he first entered it in 1902, and the developments which led to the founding of a republic.

Likewise the Arab Awakening captured his sympathy and imagination. Although he was not in favor of the form of government chosen for the new State of Iraq he co-operated wholeheartedly with its leaders after it became a *fait accompli* and was generous in advice and assistance to them all, from King Feisal and Nuri Pasha down to the humblest official.

His early tours gave him understanding of the tribes—their relation to each other, their strengths and weaknesses, and the way they fitted into the body politic.

Outside Iraq, the Palestine problem was my husband's chief concern in the Arab world. What Glubb Pasha has aptly referred to as "The Twice Promised Land" was, after the First World War, the scene of increasing tensions between Jews and Arabs. The vague statements in the Hussein-McMahon letters in 1915, the Sykes Picot Agreement in 1916, and the Balfour Declaration in 1917, could be interpreted in many different ways. In

1918, the Anglo-French declaration stated plainly that the countries liberated from Turkish rule should be free to choose their own government.

The Mandate for Palestine was allotted to Great Britain in 1922. At that time, if the conflicting promises made to Jews and Arabs could have been analyzed and the issues clarified, a reconciliation would have been possible. The two peoples had lived amicably side by side in Palestine for centuries without the least enmity. In Iraq, where the Jewish minority for the most part were descendants from the Babylonian Captivity, they had lived peaceably with the Arabs ever since. The first Minister of Finance in the new State of Iraq was a Jew, and many positions of trust in government and in the business community were held by his coreligionists.

There was goodwill on both sides, and it is one of the saddest chapters in the history of the Near East that jealousy and animosity were allowed to develop between two friendly races of the same Semitic stock, leading to bitter hatred and one of the worst trouble spots in the world today: Israel, surrounded by hostile Arab neighbors.

John Van Ess recognized and understood the problem presented by the large number of Jews coming to Palestine. The original inhabitants were augmented by many refugees from Eastern Europe. Unless a peaceful arrangement between them and the Arabs in the same area could be achieved, friction and possible conflict was inevitable.

During the Mandate, the British tried to set up a representative government in Palestine, but the Jews and Arabs in turn boycotted their efforts. Extremists on both sides resorted to terrorism and there were many political assassinations and much bloodshed. Strikes and uprisings were common. The Jews persisted in illegal immigration, and continued to build up their economic activities. The Arabs were suspicious and uneasy, as they saw the threat to their own aspirations.

In 1923 Basrah had been visited by Dr. Judah Magnes, who was to be President of the Hebrew University on Mount Scopus in Jerusalem. He was an American, a cultural Zionist, a friend of the Arabs as well as his own people. We laid the foundation then of a firm friendship with this great and good man, which lasted as long as he and John lived. They were kindred spirits, and we had the good fortune to travel on the same ship with him from Beirut to New York some years later, which gave him a chance for long leisurely discussions on subjects near to both their hearts.

In 1937 I spent the summer in America with our children, and John decided to go to Jerusalem for his vacation. He declared he was supersaturated with the Arab point of view, and wanted to live among the Jews for a while and see things from their standpoint. Dr. Magnes arranged for him to stay with the family of a German Jewish doctor, Rudolph Freund, who had been for nine years on the medical faculty of Berlin University, and then left Germany because of the rising tide of Hitlerism.

My husband saw Dr. Magnes constantly, both in his home and at the Hebrew University. He was made welcome in the circle of cultured and learned Jews who had left Europe and taken temporary refuge in Palestine. There were scholars of distinction, professors, doctors, bankers, business men, and philanthropists, all animated by the highest ideals and aspirations, for their own people and the rest of mankind.

During this summer my husband also came to know leading members of the two great Arab clans, the Husseinis and the Nashashibis—unfortunately at feud with one another. He also knew the British High Commissioner, Sir Arthur Wauchope, and General Wavell and Sir John Dill. They would often send for him to come to have dinner with them, and ply him with questions as to what he was hearing from his Arab and Jewish friends.

After talking extensively with all these people and getting their different points of view, John ventured to draw up a solution for Palestine, which he called "The United States of the Near East." It was published in the Palestine *Post* on August 2, 1937, and was widely quoted. The plan included the following main points:

1. The forming of a Federation of five states: Lebanon, Syria, Jebel Druze, Israel (most of Judea, and the south country to the Gulf of Aqaba), and the rest of Palestine combined with Jordan.
2. The Federation to be bound together on the general plan of the United States of America, including a federal government located at Jerusalem.
3. The federal government to legislate for that which concerns all—including mail, communications, currency, foreign affairs, federal courts, etc.
4. The state to control affairs concerned with local matters

such as local revenues, security, education, immigration, etc.

This would do away with artificial and arbitrary boundaries, and obviate the necessity of a "corridor" to connect Jerusalem with the sea, which was proposed in many plans.

Upon the appearance of this letter in the newspaper, the high commissioner sent for John, and told him that he saw no objection to the plan, except that it was too plausible!

John sent it to the London *Times*, and received a courteous reply, saying that the editor was greatly interested to read and consider the suggestions, but felt,

". . . it could hardly be published with effect at present. The solution propounded is a little remote from present conditions and would have a better chance if it were put forward at a later stage."

Sir Arnold Wilson, now a member of Parliament, tried again later to have the letter printed in the London *Times*, and made a vigorous attempt to present the suggestions to the House of Commons, but was unsuccessful.

Nuri Pasha Said was in substantial agreement with the general plan, which I know he and John often discussed together. He proposed a very similar plan at a Parliamentary Conference on Palestine in October, 1938.

We went to Jerusalem again for our summer holiday in 1939, and found conditions much worse than they had been when John was there in 1937. We lived in a house rented by the Anglican Cathedral authorities for Archdeacon Stewart (later Bishop Stewart). It was on Salah el Din Road, in a Moslem quarter, and was owned by a member of the Husseini family. No Jewish taxis were willing to come directly to the house, so when we wanted to go over to the other side of town to visit our Jewish friends, we had to walk through to Nablus Road, on which the Cathedral and St. George's School were located. Our dry cleaners, a Jewish company, wouldn't deliver our clothes to our house—they left them at the hostel on the other road. In our privileged position as neutrals, we were free in all parts of the city, and welcome in all the different circles. There were persons of moderate opinion on both the Arab and Jewish sides who deeply regretted the state of affairs, but were powerless to check the violence of the terrorists.

During this summer one encouraging event occurred. This was the preparation of a memorandum containing a detailed and carefully worked out scheme for bringing Arabs and Jews together in peaceful co-operation. Mr. Julius Simon, a prominent New York businessman, wished to have it considered by a group of sponsors, among whom he hoped to include Mr. Louis D. Brandeis, Justice Felix Frankfurter and Professor Albert Einstein, the Marquis of Reading, M. Leon Blum, and other Jews of distinction and influence. There was to be a small working committee including some non-Jewish members, and Mr. Simon asked my husband to be one of them. Unfortunately the outbreak of World War Two prevented the carrying out of this plan, which might have settled the problem in a constructive way.

Throughout the war the whole question was put aside. In 1947 the United Nations sent a committee of enquiry to Palestine, as Britain had announced that she was surrendering the Mandate in May, 1948.

John and I were again spending the summer in Palestine, and went to some of the hearings presented to the commission. The Arabs boycotted it, in the same unrealistic way that they had boycotted a Royal Commission in 1937. The only voice raised on their behalf was that of the Anglican Bishop Stewart.

Our friend Dr. Magnes proposed to the Commission a plan to which we listened with deepest interest. It was a bi-partite state, with equal rights and duties for both Jews and Arabs, to be united with Trans-Jordan, Syria, and Lebanon in an economic political federation, which in turn would be part of a union of free nations. Someone said that Dr. Magnes was the most Christian-like person in the country, and that if everyone had been like him, there would have been no Palestine problem. Certainly his idealistic and conciliatory spirit was uncongenial to extremists on both sides. He and John had melancholy discussions together in the following weeks; both were in failing health and had not many years to live. It was heartbreaking for Dr. Magnes to see the collapse of all his hopes for his people, and the bitter fighting of the following year between Jews and Arabs was a tragedy for everyone concerned.

After the distressing period following the arbitrary formation of the State of Israel, the refugee problem became acute, especially in Jordan, where many of the unfortunate displaced Arabs had been sent. John had a scheme for locating at least some of them in Iraq, which is underpopulated, and has large areas available for raising sheep. The Arabs of Palestine were also a pastoral people, and could easily have adjusted in this very similar environment. This project sounded reasonable and practical, and was agreed to in theory by many responsible persons, but like so many other constructive ideas, it fell afoul of political considerations and nothing came of it.

John did not live to see the Iraqi Revolution of 1958, but how often, during those dark days, I remembered hearing him say to well-born young Iraqis,

"If you don't do something about the underprivileged on your land and in your towns, some day you are going to have a revolution on your hands."

I had known in a vague way that he thought there might be economic uprisings, but I was shaken to realize the accuracy of his political predictions.

My husband's scholarship was recognized far beyond the confines of our mission area. Professor Clay of Yale, on one of his visits to Iraq, urged John to make a scientific study of some of the dialects of the Marsh Arabs and compare them with ancient languages of Mesopotamia. Then he was to come to Yale and write it up in a dissertation correlated with linguistic work he had already done.

"I'll see that you get your Ph.D. in a year's time," he promised.

At that time a doctor's degree was not a professional asset in Iraq, as it would be now, and John already had a B.D. and an M.A. from Princeton. He did not care to spend a whole winter in the marshes, away from his family and his school, and so he declined the offer, with thanks and appreciation.

In addition to his knowledge of Arabic, he was a fine Hebrew scholar, and he had offers of chairs in Oriental languages from both American and British universities.

His gift for preaching was often called upon in St. Peter's, Basrah, as well as in many places in America and elsewhere. He was "sounded out" in New York, as to whether he would consider a pulpit in one of the Collegiate churches of our denomination, but never gave them the least encouragement. "This one thing I do" was his slogan.

In lighter vein, John was an excellent after-dinner speaker, and I can recall vividly some of the occasions in Basrah when he responded for "The Guests" at the annual dinner of the English Society of St. George. He loved to make jokes at the expense of his British friends and they thoroughly enjoyed his good-natured banter.

In America, John was in demand as a lecturer by a wide range of secular organizations: the Foreign Policy Association, Town Hall Club, English Speaking Union, Schools of Journalism in various parts of the country, and various universities and colleges. When he was available he was always asked to attend an annual conference on the Near East, usually held in Washington.

Among my husband's secular interests, aside from politics, his love of sports was outstanding. He had played football in college, and was an expert skater and swimmer. He believed in boxing as a participant as well as a spectator, and for years had a special boxing instructor in the School of High Hope. He said it did the boys good to work off steam by putting on a pair of boxing gloves, and having a legitimate outlet for their energy. He greatly enjoyed watching boxing, wrestling matches, and prize-fights. On one occasion he had been giving a lecture on missions at Princeton Seminary, and the wife of one of the professors asked him afterwards,

"Won't you come to our house to supper, Mr. Van Ess, and go to prayer-meeting with us in the evening?"

To which he replied seriously,

"Thank you very much, Mrs. Blank, but I have an important engagement in New York, and I'm off to catch my train."

The important engagement was to go to a prize-fight at Madison Square Garden!

He loved horses, and knew a good deal about them. He greatly enjoyed the horse-racing in Basrah, during a period when there was a race-track and a regular program. An American visitor who went with him to the races was amazed at how many winners he picked, and remarked enviously,

"What a pity, Mr. Van Ess, that you are not a betting man! You might have made a lot of money for your school."

John's great love in the field of sports was baseball. He played it himself as a boy and a young man, and followed professional baseball all his life with keenest interest. In the days before radio, he received the sports editions of newspapers regularly by mail. Whenever he was in America he attended games if at all possible, and took his children with him and indoctrinated them at an early age. A favorite story in our family annals is of an

incident that took place in New York during the Second World
War.

The State Department was consulting John regularly about
events in the Near East, often over the telephone and frequently
by personal interviews in New York or Washington. One summer afternoon they called our home on Morningside Drive, and
my black domestic helper told them that neither Mr. nor Mrs.
Van Ess was at home. They tried my office (I was working for
our mission headquarters at this time) and were told that I was
out of town on a speaking engagement. My secretary gave them
our daughter's telephone number, at her place of work down on
Wall Street.

"Miss Van Ess, we *must* get in touch with your father," said
an urgent voice from Washington. "Have you any idea where he
is?"

"I'm sorry, I don't know," replied his daughter. "He might
be somewhere in the Columbia Library, or at the Faculty
Club."

In a short time she had another agitated message. In the
meantime she had had an inspiration. She was as ardent a
baseball fan as her father, and she looked in the daily paper and
saw that the New York Giants were playing the Chicago Cubs at
the Polo Grounds. The Cubs were her father's favorites.

"I think he may be at the ball game," she informed the
person at the other end.

Accordingly Washington called the office at the Polo
Grounds and asked them to page Dr. John Van Ess.

"We never page anyone at the Polo Grounds," was the curt
answer.

They were told that this was government business, connected
with the war and extremely important, and that they must
comply.

So John was located, and with very bad grace left his seat and
went to the telephone.

"Can you come to Washington as soon as possible, Dr. Van
Ess?" said the voice speaking for the State Department, with a
brief explanation of the crisis.

"No, I can't!" answered my husband bluntly. "I have a very
full schedule, and I am not well. If it is so important, send
someone up here and I'll be glad to talk with him. The trains
run both ways."

The ruling passion of John Van Ess's life was expressed in the verse: "And ye shall know the truth and the truth shall make you free."

His faith was deep and vital, and he exulted in every achievement of man in discovering new facts about the universe. He was thrilled by the progress of aviation during his lifetime, and he would have been profoundly moved by the exploration of outer space in recent years. He used to say that God is far greater than any conception which man can have of Him, and that each new discovery in science adds to our puny and limited knowledge of truth.

One of his friends at Princeton wrote of him:

"He had a razor-like mind, a hatred of sham, and a passion for reality."

This was apropos of an occasion when he had been asked to lead the daily chapel service at Princeton Theological Seminary. He went to the reading desk and opened the Bible, and read the story of the Good Samaritan in this way:

A certain man went down from New York to Philadelphia, and fell among thieves, which stripped him of his raiment and wounded him, and departed leaving him half dead. And by chance there came down a certain Presbyterian elder that way; and when he saw him, he passed by on the other side, for he had a committee at the church on how to stimulate interest in benevolences. And likewise a Presbyterian minister, when he was at the place, came and looked on him, and passed by on the other side, for he had to hurry on to Philadelphia to give an address over the radio on brotherly love. But a certain Communist, as he journeyed, came where he was; and when he saw him, he had compassion on him, and went to him, and bound up his wounds, pouring in mercurochrome, and set him in his Ford car, and brought him to a hospital in Philadelphia, and took care of him. And on the morrow when he departed, he took out some bills and gave them to the superintendent, and said unto him, "Take care of him: and whatsoever thou spendest more, when I come again, I will repay thee." Which now of these three, thinkest thou, was neighbor unto him that fell among the thieves?

This was a daring way to read Scripture, and a salutary one. Some of his hearers were amused, some felt prickings of conscience, and many were frankly shocked. One good man said, after he had walked out of the chapel,

"That was a terrible thing to do. Sacrilegious. If only he had not chosen the Communist as the shining example."

Probably the Jews said the same thing after Jesus finished his story.

"If only he hadn't chosen a Samaritan for the hero of his tale!" not realizing that he purposely took the most despised person, because he wanted to disturb the complacency of the respectable and conventional members of society.

An apt characterization of my husband was written during his lifetime by one of our short-termers, J. Coert Rylaarsdam, now a professor at the Divinity School at the University of Chicago. He called it:

John Van Ess: Builder of a Christian World.

There are some men who possess true versatility. They enjoy the hurly-burly of the marketplace as much as the solemnity of the desert. Their advice and company is sought by the cultured and mighty, yet the illiterate nomad group becomes sociable when they join it. They rebuke with stinging sarcasm and encourage with comforting tenderness. They have wisdom for the wise and understanding of the foolish. They respond with equal alacrity to a host of situations, but never cease to be themselves. Such a man is John Van Ess.

For more than thirty years, Dr. Van Ess has lived in Arabia at the crossroads of cultures and civilizations. In Basrah he has lived under four flags. He has travelled on donkeys and rafts of skins, but also by train and plane. He has outwitted Turkish governors, and been snubbed by their policemen. The British Intelligence Service has thanked him for corrective data, and smiled at his advice. For years he has taught the alphabet to barefoot boys, and gone home to write Arabic grammars and textbooks. Arabs have hung on his lips as he told them the story and meaning of Jesus, and Christians have refused to listen to him. But he is still John Van Ess, a gentleman, an ambassador of Christ, independent, unpredictable.

He looks up from a new version of *Mashakilu es-Shubaan—The Problems of Young Men*, to greet an Arab who has come to ask his help in finding work. He is stern: "But what

about the job I got you last week? It was burdensome, was it?
What an affront to come back to me! You have destroyed my
honour with your last employer. Don't you think there are any
limits to God's mercy?" And he continues with a withering
invective against all that is shiftless and spineless. Then with a
sigh he leaves the room, telephones, and intercedes for another
job.

The grateful, hand-kissing Arab has hardly left when Dr. Van
Ess reflects, "I suppose they think me an easy mark. But I was
thinking of those hungry children at home. They will smile
when Baba returns with the news that he has work again. At
least I shall be able to enjoy my own meal today. What breaks
my heart in this land is the lot of its children; their eyes grow
dull too soon; they expect so much and get so little. And we
have so much! That poem of Vachel Lindsay, *The Leaden-eyed*,
makes me weep:

> It is the world's one crime its babes grow dull,
> Its poor are ox-like, limp and leaden-eyed . . .
> Not that they serve, but have no gods to serve,
> Not that they die, but that they die like sheep.

John Van Ess is stern, tactful, and diplomatic. But he is
above all human and powerful in his sympathies. During the
recent years in which Iraq has been emerging as a nation, Dr.
Van Ess has been in the thick of national life. He has not
participated directly in politics, but his advice has been sought
by high and low.

At night Dr. Van Ess sits under the stars, relaxed in the
limpid, cozy, tropical night, and he sighs with a sigh in which
are contained all the burdens of the world. For the sorrows of
the sad are his burden, and the emptiness of the underprivileged
his need. But on the morrow he walks erect and laughs at the
awkwardness of his cross-eyed servant. He is full of fun, for he
has found a new way out once more. Or rather, the old way in a
new pattern: Christ, the hope of the world.

XVII
Epilogue

Our life together was finished, and I was by myself. Once again I had to face the tremendous psychological and spiritual readjustments of bereavement, only this time I was alone.

For a week I was in Basrah, encompassed by the affection and helpfulness of the mission circle there. I was fortified by the many expressions of sympathy for me and tributes to John that I received from high and low, near and far. A cable from Washington signed "Acheson," who was then Secretary of State, pleased me very much. So did a letter to my husband from Nuri Pasha Said, which I found in a pocket of the coat John had been wearing on his last afternoon with us. This expressed Nuri's gratitude for forty-seven years of service for the good of the people of Iraq and wished him well. I was so glad this letter had come while John was here to read it.

I went to Baghdad, and from there took the Taurus Express, and travelled through the famed Cilician Gates in Central Turkey. I stayed with friends in Ankara and in Istanbul, in heavenly spring weather, and then flew to England, where I spent most of the summer.

Once back in America, of course, my first wish was to be with family and friends. My daughter met me at the airport, and I went to Washington with her. Her husband, William Brewer, was taking a course in Arabic and the Near East at the Foreign Service Institute, in preparation for going overseas again as an "area specialist." Alice and Bill were soon assigned to Jidda, in Saudi Arabia. The month before they left we spent with Bill's parents, Arnold and Cornelia Brewer, in their lovely country home in Ridgefield, Connecticut. They made me welcome as one of the family circle and have done so ever since.

After the young Brewers had departed for the Arab world, I made my headquarters with my sister, Helen Firman Sweet. I had several things to occupy me. John had been asked, shortly before our retirement was due, to be a special consultant to the State Department on the Near East in general and Iraq in particular. There was part of his first assignment which I was qualified to carry out, and it was very good for me to be working on something objective, and to have to meet a deadline.

A problem which was on my mind all the time, was to decide about my future. John and I would have gone to New Brunswick, New Jersey, one of our denominational headquarters, and spent a year at least, probably settling there permanently. I had no interest whatever now in setting up a home without him. Bill and Alice were now in Saudi Arabia, in the American Embassy at Jidda. The mission had urged me to return to the field, and I still had some years left before reaching retirement age. In talking it over with my sister, I said,

"It would seem an awful anti-climax to go back to Basrah without John," and she made one of the wisest remarks I have ever heard.

"All the rest of your life is going to be an anti-climax without John."

Accordingly I returned to the Near East in the early summer of 1950. I spent several months with my daughter in the lovely mountain village of Brummanna in Lebanon, revelling in the prospect of the curved coastline and the deep blue Mediterranean below us—to my mind almost the most beautiful view in the world. My first grandchild, John Van Ess Brewer, was born in the American University Hospital in Beirut on July 30th. This was my birthday too, and we felt that my grandson showed a fine sense of timing. We had a most happy summer, with Bill joining his family for a month; in October we went our several ways, Alice and the baby back to Jidda, and I to Basrah.

As soon as I arrived and settled down, I knew that I had made the right decision, and that this was the place where I wanted to be. The pattern of life was changed, but I was in familiar surroundings with tried and true friends, and there was work for me to do. The sense of "belonging" is very important to anyone bereft of her life companion, and so is the opportunity to be useful.

The work that lay ready to my hand was to cooperate again in our program for underprivileged girls which from small beginnings had become a large organized work. Christine Gosselink and I had worked happily together for many years, often with the welcome addition of a younger colleague—Ruth Luidens, Evelyn MacNeill, or Louise Holler—and to join them in the familiar routine was balm to my spirit.

Dorothy Van Ess and her club girls.

The story of its development was like that of Topsy, it just grew. Many years before, I had a Sunday school for the small Arab boys and girls in a little village near us, which was held after the morning service in our mission church. The numbers were not large and the program was a simple one, lasting less than an hour.

One summer John and I conducted a Daily Vacation Bible School on the boy's school compound for poor Arab boys, helped by some of our teachers, and it was literally a howling success. The program lasted between two and three hours and included organized play and gymnastics, hand work, Bible stories, health and habit talks, and other features of all DVBS activities the world around.

That autumn the Sunday crowd had grown so large that it had to be divided and the boys handed over to some of the school staff. It occurred to us that the girls, now coming in increasing numbers, would profit by an expanded program. A weekday would suit them as well as Sunday which means nothing to a Muslim, and we could work more intimately with these ragged and sometimes unhygienic youngsters if we were not dressed in our Sunday clothes!

The Thursday club was begun then and has continued ever since. In a few years the older girls were given a different day and in a few years more we had a Tuesday and a Wednesday group, as well as the large vociferous crowd of small children and beginners. Sewing was added to the "course" and eventually knitting for older girls.

At one time we had a Girl Scout program for our older girls, worked out by our English friend Joy Dowson. She divided them into four patrols, each with its own color of the rainbow. They had competitive sports and received points for neatness, order, singing, handwork, and general deportment. This taught them the value of team work, which all Arabs so greatly need, and was also excellent training in leadership and responsibility. The adding up of the points at the end of the session and discovering which patrol had won the banner for the week was the high spot of the day and evoked cheers and groans.

As the years went by we had a literacy program for girls with aptitude, desire, and the time to spend on it, and had very rewarding results.

Many of the poor girls who came to us were under economic pressure and could with difficulty be spared even for one morning a week. They had to help with the housework, the marketing, and the care of younger brothers and sisters, and some even held jobs. They worked in more affluent households for pitifully small sums; and in the date season many of them were seasonal workers in the date packing camps. Girls came to us from all parts of the section of Basrah called Ashar, and from many little settlements up and down the creeks which intersect the whole city. Daughters of our original girls were now enrolled and we had friends all over the countryside.

One of the most satisfying features was friendship with the

mothers, and we always received a warm welcome in the homes of present and former pupils. How pleasant it was, on a brisk winter afternoon, to go into one of their mat huts, where a rug was spread out, with neat covered cushions to lean against as we sat on the floor; the flowered teapot hospitably ready, and the tea glasses set out on a tray. Friends and neighbors crowded sociably in from the courtyard, and our young hostesses and their mothers liked us to bring our knitting, because when we got it out, they felt we were settling down for a good long visit. Many of the mothers and grandmothers, and other relatives and friends, came to our Christmas programs, sewing exhibits, special film showings like *The King of Kings*, and other gatherings of interest. Some of them profited secondhand from the lessons on child care and family life which now formed part of our schedule for the older girls. The girls had an annual Sports Day which was a great affair, and in the spring we often arranged a picnic out on the desert.

I went to Jidda in December of 1950 to help my grandson celebrate his first Christmas. I shall always be glad that I saw the city of our Mother Eve ("Jidda" means grandmother in Arabic) and the reputed site of her tomb, while it was still a little Arab seaport and not yet modernized. The tall old houses with their balconies and lattices looked like something out of the *Arabian Nights*, and the sign a few miles up the road to Mecca, "Forbidden to all but Muslims," enhanced the sense of mystery.

In 1952 my son-in-law was transferred to the American Legation (soon to be an Embassy) in Damascus. If the State Department had asked me what post I would choose for him (they didn't) that would have been the one. That fabulous old city, with the streams of running water, its encircling fruit orchards, the famous old buildings, and the enthralling bazaars, is surely one of the choicest spots on earth. A center of Arab culture and learning, steeped in the traditions of centuries, it is the very essence of the Arab world. Henceforth, I spent each Christmas and each summer there while I was in my last term of service in Basrah. In June, 1952, my second grandson, Daniel Arnold Brewer, was born in Victoria Hospital of the Edinburgh Medical Mission in Damascus.

For the last two years before I retired, I was Mission Secretary, as I had been once before. This involved, among other duties, the pleasant opportunity of visiting each one of our mission stations: Amarah, Kuwait, Bahrain, and Muscat. My last mission meeting was in Muscat, late in 1954, and I travelled down from Basrah all the way by ship, on the good old B.I., as we always called the British India Navigation Company. The Gulf ports, with the hustle and bustle and shouting, as little harbor boats brought passengers and freight out to the steamer, were as beguiling to me as they had been on my first voyage so many years ago. The medley of color and noise and smells delighted me, and the assorted humanity was of absorbing interest to me, as it always has been.

The pangs of my last months in Basrah, in 1955, were greatly softened for me by the knowledge that Bill was going to be sent to Kuwait to be in charge of the American Consulate.

There was a pleasant series of farewell parties, and I left Basrah Airport with a lovely gold "Ship of Love" brooch pinned to my lapel, the gift of the members of the Arab Christian Women's Society. I went to Damascus and helped my family pack up for Kuwait, and then spent the rest of the summer in Jerusalem.

When I returned to Kuwait, it was to live in the spacious Arab mansion on the seashore which contained the Consulate and the living quarters of the consul and his family. From the broad verandahs we had an incomparable view of the Persian Gulf and all the shipping, and the seagulls wheeling and soaring before us. Kuwait was no longer the quiet little Arab town I had known in my early years, for the oil industry had made it one of the most important ports in the Near East. It was growing by leaps and bounds, but the city walls had not yet been demolished, and boats were still being built along the sea front. I was very content to be in one of our own mission stations; our hospitals were flourishing and our church ministered to many different nationalities, brought in by the growing industrial developments.

I had a piece of work to do, which was ideal for a newly retired missionary. My colleagues had asked me to write the history of the mission for the last thirty years, since the previous official history had been published in the 1920's. There was a wealth of material to draw from, in our missionary magazines, annual reports, special pamphlets, and the delightful "Golden Milestone," written by our founders, Samuel Zwemer and James Cantine, for our 50th anniversary. I had the advantage of being able to consult all our members in the different stations as I worked, and to pay frequent visits to Basrah. I circulated the first draft around the whole mission for corrections and suggestions before I left the field. It was a wonderfully satisfying experience to go over the record of those years in a leisurely way and share in the varied activities of my friends and fellow workers. I found the accounts of touring especially fascinating, perhaps because I had spent my years in educational work in one place. These tales of pioneering by camel, sailboat, and donkey in Saudi Arabia and in Oman (and later by car) held me spellbound.

The great event of our family life in Kuwait was the birth of Priscilla Joan Brewer in January, 1956. Her christening in the mission church was a memorable occasion, with our English friend, the Reverend Harold Adkins (now Canon Adkins) over from Jerusalem to officiate, assisted by the Reverend Don MacNeill of our own mission. She wore a christening robe which had been in Bill's family for several generations, as her brothers had done, with the feminine addition of tiny gold bracelets given to her mother by my school girls in Basrah when she was a new baby.

In the spring of 1956 I left the Near East to return to America, but without the usual "retirement blues," because I felt sure that the door was not closed and that I would return. The Brewers now had a Washington assignment.

The Iraqi Revolution in 1958 was a terrible shock. I heard of it in Chicago over the radio on the morning of that fateful fourteenth of July and could hardly believe my ears as the tale of violence unfolded. The world had considered Iraq one of the most stable of the Arab countries, and so it was as long as Nuri el Said was at the helm. I was very sad at his tragic death. It was the irony of fate that he who had been one of the earliest leaders in the "Arab awakening," should have been assassinated as a reactionary. The rising generation were impatient with what they considered the slowness of the older statesmen who had been in power so long, and the young intelligentsia in the army had been anti-royalist for some years.

The military organization which had staged the coup d'etat and seized power, with Brigadier Abdul Kerim Kassim at their head, was now established and proclaimed the Republic of Iraq. Russian influence had been at work, and for a time the outside world wondered if the young Republic would "go Communist."

The members of our missions were not in immediate personal danger, but many of them were ordered out of the country summarily, especially the ones in northern Iraq. Our doctors were sent out of Amarah, and the whole mission property there (hospital, houses, and church) was confiscated. Curiously enough, our schools in Basrah and Baghdad have never been disturbed by the new regime.

In 1959 I went to spend the academic year in New York. I had long had a book about Arab women "in my system," and I felt that I would be paying a debt of gratitude for my rich experiences in their world, if I sorted it out and set it down. I worked at Columbia University under the great anthropologist, Margaret Mead, and had the inestimable benefit of her keen interest and close supervision as I wrote *Fatima and Her Sisters*. This was the title John had selected for the chapter about women in his *Meet the Arab*, and it seemed a natural choice for my book. The John Day Company published it in 1961, and my friends and the general public seemed to enjoy reading it as much as I had enjoyed writing it.

In the fall of 1963 I had my long anticipated return to Basrah. My "base" was now Afghanistan, where my son-in-law had been assigned after five years in the State Department in Washington. He was now Deputy Chief of Mission in the American Embassy in Kabul, and I joined the family there late in 1962. I spent the following summer in Lebanon and Jerusalem, and as soon as autumn came I went to Kuwait for a few days and then to Basrah.

Enough time had passed since the Revolution so that the nationals of Iraq had become less guarded in their attitude toward foreigners. Our schools were flourishing and little girls had come back to our clubs in considerable numbers. I had known that I would have a hearty welcome from the Gosselinks and the other missionaries in Basrah, but I was not in the least prepared for the warmth of the welcome I had from all my Arab friends. It was one of the most wonderful experiences of my life. In the all-too-short five weeks I was there, I never felt the least constraint between myself and any of my Iraqi friends. They made the advances in every case, as I had made up my mind that I would be very cautious in re-establishing my relationships with all nationals.

Old pupils of John's and mine came and called on me and

hailed me with delight if we met elsewhere. When I went for the first time to see my Hajjia to whom I had dedicated *Fatima*, we embraced and then we both burst into tears from happiness and emotion.

The government was still not stable and no one felt sure of what would happen from one day to the next. Abdul Kerim Kassim had been assassinated in his turn, and the newest regime seemed very shaky. Two hours after I had left Baghdad Airport for Teheran in November there was yet another coup, and the airport was closed. The government since then has seemed steady and has pursued an even course. Iraq was represented at the Conference of Arab States in Cairo, and there is much discussion of Arab unity. Only the future can disclose how this great people will continue to work out their destiny.

I have had a good life. As it draws to its close my feelings are well expressed by the traditional "Old Age Prayer." This has been used by Sunni and Shiah Muslims from the time of Abd al Qadir al Jilani (1166 A.D.) and was quoted as the prayer of an Arab overheard by the Prophet in passing:

"O Lord, may the end of my life be the best of it,
may my closing acts be my best acts,
and make the best of my days the day when I shall meet
Thee."